For Millie Somers,

Who loved enough once to last a million lifetimes,
and whose example gives us all the ability to live and love
fully and forever.

1,001 Ways to Have a Dazzling Second Wedding

By

Sharon Naylor

NEW PAGE BOOKS
A division of The Career Press, Inc.
Franklin Lakes, NJ

1,001 Ways to Have a Dazzling Second Wedding
Cover design by Tom Phon
Typesetting by Eileen Munson
Printed in the U.S.A. by Book-mart Press

To order this title, please call toll-free 1-800-CAREER-1 (NJ and Canada: 201-848-0310) to order using VISA or MasterCard, or for further information on books from Career Press.

The Career Press, Inc., 3 Tice Road, PO Box 687,
Franklin Lakes, NJ 07417
www.careerpress.com
www.newpagebooks.com

ISBN: 1-56414-520-4
Library of Congress Cataloging-in-Publication Data available upon request.

Acknowledgments

I'd like to thank so many people for their help with this book:

First of all, my agent, Elizabeth Frost Knappman, for her guidance of this project.

My editors, Mikc Lcwis, Karen Prager, and Stacey Farkas, and the creative team at Career Press, for the professional treatment of my material.

Beth Reed Ramirez, editor of *Bride Again* magazine, for her wonderful interviews and her willingness to share not only information on the current trends in the wedding industry, but on her own second wedding experience as well.

Shirley Feuerstein of Affairs and Arrangements, for always returning my calls, answering my questions, and guiding me along new paths.

Rich Penrose at Dean Michaels Studios, for his reliability, his wonderful artistry, his vision, and his generosity.

Steve Blahitka of Back East Productions, for his technical know-how, his support of the project, and his highly creative productions. What a talent, and what a future!

Henry Weinreich of Michelle Roth Studios, for making time in his busy schedule to point out the best in bridal fashions. Henry, save that pink English gown with the flowers at the back for me.

Sylvia Weinstock, for her amazing craftsmanship with cakes and frostings, and her staff's willingness and efficiency in sending pictures that were pretty enough to eat.

Angela Lanzafame of The Potted Geranium, for all of her help with my many projects.

Gail Watson, for her quick sending of her favor and groom's cake materials.

Laura Schmidt, Tara Bruno, and Julie Weingarden, the best up-and-coming writers in the industry.

Joanne Blahitka, who dictated a chapter to me when my computer crashed right before deadline, and whose unsung support makes her an angel in the eyes of those who count.

Karen Beyke, for her legal and contract expertise.

Andrew Blahitka, for his quiet support of my work, and for his expressions of caring and pride in my accomplishment. And thanks for building my new desk! You are the master creator.

Paula Bortnichak and Lenore Millian, for their insightful relationship counseling advice.

And to my wonderful family, true friends, and illuminating mentors.

"In life, everyone gets a
second chance."
— Sharon Naylor

❧

"It's never too late to be what
you might have been."
—George Eliot

Contents

Foreword

The Second-Time Jitters

This is certainly a very exciting time in your life—so much to do, so much to plan, all of the joy and anticipation of picturing your wedding day, having a new future to embark upon. Although any new bride experiences the typical jitters, yours—as a second-time bride—may be a bit more intense. Perhaps you've had a failed first marriage, and you fear that this union too might not last. If you are widowed, you may be experiencing some guilt or fears about marrying again.

You may be remembering your first wedding at every turn, remembering the vows you took with your first husband and wondering about the validity of vows in the first place. After all, you vowed to love, honor, and respect for all eternity. Can anyone make a promise like that? Can vows be taken seriously? These types of questions can swirl in your head, causing even the most committed bride to question the institution of marriage.

It's completely normal to feel this way now. Every second-time bride does. In fact, it would be simplistic and unrealistic to tell you to put it out of your mind, because you're not going to be able to do that. These are legitimate issues, legitimate concerns, and it's best to deal with them now. If you do not, you'll repress your feelings, only to have them come tumbling down upon you as you're walking down the aisle on your wedding day. Let's take them one at a time, get them out of the way, so that you can enjoy your wedding and start a new life with a clear and confident mind:

Jitters over a failed first marriage

If your first marriage failed, you're likely to have some thoughts about that right now. Most brides I've spoken to say their thoughts ranged from "I never thought on my first wedding day that I'd ever be divorced from my husband" to "What if this marriage ends too?" These brides say that they spent a lot of time thinking back over the good and bad moments of their first marriage, and that they were afraid that they couldn't handle it if this marriage went south as well.

Again, it's normal to feel this way. You've experienced a great loss in your life, and it's going to be hard to keep that out of your mind as you prepare yourself to begin a life with a new partner. But don't make the mistake of boiling it all down to an issue of marriage on/marriage off. What you should be thinking about is this: *You are a completely different person now than you were in your first marriage.* The person you are now is not going to make the same mistakes or endure the same treatment as the person you used to be did. This is very important for you to see right now, so that you can look at your marriage not as a walk down the same path again, but as a walk down a new path as a new person.

Very often, from the end of a first marriage comes a period of growth and learning. In reestablishing your own identity, after you broke from the identity you had during your marriage, you have undoubtedly strengthened your own sense of self. Perhaps in becoming your own person again, you've tapped into your hidden talents and developed positive traits that have made you a better, stronger person, one better suited to making a marriage work with a good partner.

What you've gained are the following:

- Loss of naivete.
- Loss of submissive behavior.
- Ability to think of your own needs.
- Ability to think of self and partner as equals.
- Having more self-esteem.

This is particularly the case if you married young the first time. Now, you're older and wiser, you may have more of an identity of your own, and perhaps a strong sense of yourself as connected to your work. With all of this growth and change, you are better suited now to make a success of your marriage.

Many second-time brides are actually *thankful* that their first marriages ended. They acknowledge that they weren't truly happy during that first union, and that even through the painful period of ending it, they have experienced a full blooming of themselves. They have learned lessons that they couldn't have learned otherwise, and now they have the insight they need to have a better marriage and a better future. Their failed first marriage, then, was a blessing.

If you still have jitters at this point, if you fear that this marriage too will end, you may need to take some action now. The best thing you can do is try to identify what went wrong during your first marriage. This isn't always easy, because it's usually fault on both partner's parts that contributes to the end of a marriage. What you can do to prevent yourself from making the same mistakes again is to spell out what you might have done wrong the first time that you're going to have to work hard not to do again.

1. Acknowledge that you may have played at least a small part in the end of the marriage.

2. Look at your reactions to the things your ex did wrong. Could you have reacted differently? Did you overreact? Did you under-react?

3. Looking back now, what would you have done differently, and what would you have done the same?

This is a difficult exercise, as it requires looking into your own shortcomings. But it can also reinforce to you that yes, you did do the right things sometimes. And when you can objectively see what you did wrong—perhaps you nagged too much or you didn't listen fully to your partner all the time—you can identify a problem that has to be worked on. That is half the battle right there, and it is a crucial step that you can take to avoid the same mistakes from being replayed in the second marriage.

This by no means suggests that you are to take on all blame for the end of the marriage, that you're to look only for what you did wrong. Your first husband was a part of the marriage, and he had a hand in the end of it as well. Before we get into the next step, assessing the mistakes to avoid in this marriage, thereby assuaging your jitters about getting married again, I will encourage you to also look at what your ex did wrong, what mistakes he made. As you truly delve into these thoughts, you will see that *you just weren't a good fit*. Perhaps neither of you had the right ability levels of communication or the right role models, or the right levels of maturity and commitment that is needed for marriage at that time. As you go through the list below, you're not only looking to see where you stumbled, but where your partner stumbled. You will then make an honest effort not to repeat these mistakes, perhaps finding that you never would again, and, as most brides do, use the list to finally realize that you have grown, you have stopped bad behaviors, your new partner does not make these mistakes, and that you and he *are* a good fit.

The most common mistakes in a failed marriage are:

- Not listening to your partner.
- Not taking your partner's needs into consideration.
- Putting up with your partner's not taking *your* needs into consideration.
- Not knowing how to fight constructively.
- Trying to change your partner.
- Not speaking your mind.
- Allowing yourself to be controlled.
- Controlling your partner.
- Allowing yourself to be abused.
- Abusing your partner.
- Making your spouse your whole world.
- Acting selfishly.
- Betraying your spouse.
- Becoming submissive.
- Falling into routine.
- Not thinking of yourself and your spouse as equals.
- Subjugating yourself for your partner's needs.
- Having low self-esteem.
- Becoming too dependent upon your spouse.
- Manipulating or lying to your partner.
- Withholding secrets about your past.
- Letting your spouse get away with things.

These are some of the many mistakes that can be made in a marriage. Think about others that you might have experienced, and then consciously think about how to *not* make these same mistakes again. Your efforts, and your spouse's efforts, will help this marriage to last forever.

There is a good side to having jitters related to a failed first marriage—if you didn't love your new partner so much, you wouldn't be so afraid of this marriage not lasting forever. So adjust your perspective; you love your new husband-to-be and you're willing to do whatever it takes as the better, stronger you to make this marriage last a lifetime. Action is all it takes to knock away the jitters.

Jitters after being widowed

If your first marriage came to an end due to the death of your spouse, you're likely to experience some conflicting emotions. You love your new partner, but you may feel like you're somehow being unfaithful to your departed spouse. You took vows, after all, to be faithful to your first husband for the rest of your life, so are you going back on them now by marrying another person? Of course not. You live on, and you have a right to be happy.

Many widowed second-time brides tell me that it helps them to think that their departed spouses are happy for them now.

> "I like to think of my first husband looking down on me from heaven, smiling. And I also like to think that maybe he had something to do with my finding my new fiance, like he pulled some fate strings for me to lead us together since he knows my new fiancé is a good man and would make me happy."
>
> —Claire, 32, widow and second-time bride

If you are a widow, you may also have a strong fear of allowing yourself to love a new man and possibly risk losing this one to death as well . It's normal for you to fear a repeat of a past traumatic circumstance, but you cannot allow a fear to control your life and prevent the happiness that can be found right now. Your only choice, then, is to acknowledge that loss does happen, and you must allow yourself the freedom to live life to its fullest with the people you've been given to share it with.

Jitters related to having been there before

Most likely, with every decision you make related to the planning of your wedding, a small part of your mind is going to be saying, "I've done this before." You've tried on wedding gowns before, you've picked out flowers for a bouquet, you've interviewed caterers, and you've gone on a honeymoon. There is a real danger in coloring these steps with such a thought process, looking at them as anything less than a brand new experience. Yes, you've planned a wedding before, but this is a new you planning a meaningful ceremony and celebration to begin a new marriage and a new life together. So each step you take is a new and unique experience for you. Think of it that way.

It might also help to think of each task and each decision as an opportunity improve upon your first wedding. This is not to say that you should create a horserace between your first wedding and your second. You're not trying to one-up your first wedding, because in doing so you would be making your first wedding an element in this one. That's not fair to you or to your new spouse. Instead, look at it as an opportunity to create the perfect day for who you are now, filled with everything you've ever wanted.

For many brides, their first wedding was not truly their own. In many cases, their parents were paying for the wedding, and with that status comes a strong decision-affecting power. These first-time brides may have been young, just out of school, more naïve, and willing to allow some decisions to be taken from their hands. Now, as the new and improved you, and as an independent woman who is most likely not having her parents pay for the wedding, you are more in control of the planning of your wedding. You may be a more confident person, and you may have no problem telling pushy relatives to back off and let you make the decisions yourself.

The key lies in perspective. Although it would be easy to wallow in the memories of your first wedding, you would be wise to look at it in a different sense. Consider having gone through a first wedding to be *a benefit* in the creation of this wedding. You've gone through the process before, you know which mistakes to avoid and which details to pay extra close attention to. You know how to negotiate for better service, better prices, and better options, and you know what you *don't* want for your wedding day. That kind of insight comes only from experience.

It may help you to know that most brides have even thought throughout their first marriages that they wished their weddings could have been different, that they left out something they really wanted, or that they shouldn't have tried so hard to save money for their parents. You may have felt that way too. Now you have a chance to create the wedding of your dreams on your own terms.

Jitters regarding vows

Some brides feel a pang of guilt at having to acknowledge that they didn't hold true to the original vows they made during their first marriage. Even if they had to break their vows through no fault of their own, such as the end of a marriage after a partner cheats on them, there is still a lingering feeling of uneasiness that they took a vow and couldn't hold true to it. The only way to combat this uneasiness is to acknowledge that you did the best you could. You were not alone in the marriage, and your holding true to the vows you took may not have been enough to make the marriage last forever. If by chance you didn't hold true to the vows you took, your only option is to learn from your own mistakes and judge yourself as capable of trying again. Everyone gets a second chance in life.

Your fears may focus on the validity of vows in the first place. Can someone really promise to love and cherish *forever*? Doesn't the ever-changing nature of life make that hard? Although your past may have made you a bit jaded, it's very important that you take on an optimistic side to your personality. Ask yourself this: Do you love your fiancé? Yes. Do the vows you've chosen reflect that? Of course.

The key here may be in writing your own vows, which allows you to customize your promises so that they reflect how you're really feeling. Having control over the wording of your ceremony may make you feel more confident in both of your abilities to take vows that you truly mean. And as for the fear of your vows not being able to last during the ups and downs of life, you're just going to have to believe in the best of yourself and of your partner.

This brings up a very important point. Your fear may be that your spouse will not hold up his end of the vows. If during your first marriage your spouse didn't adhere to his vows, that was surely disappointing and painful. But your new partner is not your old spouse. It would be a great mistake to transplant your fears and doubts onto this partner if he has shown you no reason why he shouldn't be trusted. Give him the credit he deserves. Don't make him pay for your ex-spouse's transgressions. Trust his sincerity and loyalty.

Just because your first vows did not hold does not mean that these won't. Remember, you're a better, stronger person on a new path with a new person. You're not going to make the same mistakes you may have made before. With these crucial elements in place, you're far more likely to have a marriage in which vows *can* be held to forever.

If you're still struggling with this issue, it might be a good idea to get some pre-marital counseling with your fiancé. He will understand that you have some issues—perhaps he has some of his own—but in the end he will realize that you are taking this step because you believe in a partnership and you want it to work out. It's something you value, so you will take steps to make sure you can be successful.

Wedding day jitters

Every bride has jitters about what might go wrong on the wedding day. We've all seen the footage on television reality shows of brides who pass out at the altar, flower girls who pitch tantrums, and even freak windstorms. If you try, you could imagine any number of catastrophes that might occur on your wedding day. The second-time bride, unfortunately, may have an extra tier of additional fears.

What if the ex-husband shows up uninvited? What if bitter relatives make comments? What if the groom's self-absorbed teenage daughter follows through on her threat to boycott the wedding? A second wedding means that guests who have been to your first wedding may be there for this one, and there may be some guests who are not blissfully happy for you this time around. Just like you can't predict the weather, you can't predict other people's actions and choices. So it does no good to worry about that which you cannot control. In a majority of cases, reality doesn't measure up to the scenarios that you can create in your mind, and you're far more likely to experience some minor problem that you didn't imagine beforehand. So don't waste your time.

Just know that whatever happens, you can handle it. Don't lock your knees at the altar, and you won't pass out. If the flower girl pitches a tantrum, just laugh and walk right by her. If Aunt Hattie is going to make a scene about etiquette breaches, just let her do it far away from you. It'll be her evening of unpleasantness, not yours.

Any number of calamities can happen at a wedding. Just smile through them. Think about the wedding scene in the movie *Betsy's Wedding*, where the rain came down and the tent broke, pouring rivers of water all over the reception. The bride laughed and looked radiant dancing barefoot in the mud, eating a slice of delivered pizza. You too can be radiant through anything, acts of God or not.

Keep your mind on the most important element of the day—that you're getting married to your best friend. You'll still be the radiant bride, and you still get to start a new life with the man of your dreams. Everything is going to go wonderfully.

The keys to fighting the jitters

- Think about what will go right, not wrong.
- Have backup plans.
- Remember to keep the focus on your marriage, not the specifics of the wedding.
- Have faith in yourself and your partner.
- Don't live in the past.
- Enjoy every moment of the planning process.
- Remember to keep a handle on your stress level.
- Know that you're a stronger person now.
- Know that you've chosen a better man.

Introduction

Congratulations on your engagement! You've found love again, and you're ready to join your lives in marriage. You have many wonderful things ahead of you now, and I have no doubt that you're glowing with radiance and anticipation of your future, showing off that dazzling engagement ring, and starting to think about the wedding you're going to have. In fact, you may already have the whole thing planned out in your mind. If so, you're like many other second-time brides who are more thrilled about this wedding than they were about their first.

Looking back on the first wedding

Most first weddings, after all, are big, glitzy affairs with the fantasy backdrop and all of the million little details that make up the stereotypical dream wedding. A first-time bride may be young, just out of school or a few years into establishing her own identity, and she may be somewhat starry-eyed about the whole prospect of planning her wedding. Her parents may be footing the entire bill, so there is a great deal of push-and-pull about the decision-making process. First-timers overwhelmingly report that they got a lot of "I'm paying for it, so it's my decision" from parents who took over many aspects of the planning. Rules of etiquette may have been forced down their throats, and the guest list was more a collection of the parents' friends than the bride's and groom's. First-time brides are stressed and worried, nervous wrecks, or they are angry that their day is not truly their own.

As you think back on your first wedding, ask yourself if it was truly your vision. Where did you have to give up control? Was it everything you wanted? What didn't work out the way you had planned? Was it *you*? There will be no avoiding looking back at the first wedding, not necessarily in sentimentality if you have been divorced, but as a comparison of sorts. Some brides want everything different from their first wedding, with no trace of similarity. Others want to incorporate some of the elements that worked, but to avoid those that no longer suit their styles.

It's not going to be the same this time

One of the most common responses from second-time brides whom I've spoken to is that this wedding planning process is unbelievably more enjoyable. The couple is older, more mature, and because they are paying for this wedding they are not under the thumb of the parental masters with the golden checkbook. The decisions are theirs to do as they please, and they do appreciate the freedom of creating their own day according to their own styles and tastes.

Shirley Feuerstein, a professional wedding coordinator with Affairs and Arrangements in New Jersey, says that second-time brides are more into the meaning of the day than all the accoutrements. They fill their ceremony and reception with personal touches, so that the wedding is a reflection of their love and their personalities to a much greater degree than first-time brides'. As a result, second-time brides create more touching and endearing weddings.

The bride and groom themselves are older, wiser, and more sophisticated and secure in their likes and dislikes. They may have an education in fine wines and a taste for exotic foods and more sophisticated music. The guest list is also a reflection of their own identities, with fewer of their parents' friends and clients and more of their own friends and clients. In short, second weddings are more evolved than first weddings. Because the couple may have gone through the entire process of planning a wedding before, as young first-timers with virtually no experience in what amounts to event-planning, their first attempt may have been affected by a following-the-crowd influence. First-timers often make decisions based on what they think is acceptable, what their parents and families want, what they see in magazines, and what the professionals tell them to do. Wedding professionals have told me that first-time couples are often taken advantage of by unscrupulous vendors who push for larger purchases and cookie-cutter design.

You're so much more advantaged than that! You've grown since then. You're making the decisions. You're calling the shots. You have the golden checkbook, and all of the details are up to you. You're no longer intimidated by what others tell you to do, and you are far more likely to stand your ground or compromise only when logical to do so. As Leah Ingram, author of *Your Wedding Your Way* says, "Now, you have better skills for communication with your family and with wedding vendors. You know how to handle issues and avoid crisis. You know how to choose your battles. Whereas during the first wedding, everything was a control issue and a highly-charged emotional decision, now you can handle each issue with a better ability to measure its importance."

You're smart enough to remove the more frivolous parts of your wedding plans, incorporate more personal ones, and use your skills and smarts to create the wedding you truly want. This time, you'll have no unspoken disappointments. You won't be pushed around. Your parents will be guests, not creative controllers. This will be your wedding, yours and your partner's, and you'll begin your married life with a celebration that comes right from your heart.

The groom's involvement

Another trend that second-time brides face is the new involvement of grooms in the wedding planning process. Gone are the days when the groom just shows up in his tux and goes where he's told. Now, grooms are taking an active part in the planning of weddings. According to Diane Forden, editor of *Bridal Guide* magazine, men are taking a big interest in plans, especially if this is their first wedding and it's your second. First-time grooms are arranging the rentals, checking out reception halls, planning honeymoons, designing the rings, choosing the menus, and even interviewing officiants. It is today's bride's good luck that men are so interested in helping to plan their own celebrations, as we are more busy with our jobs and with our family responsibilities. The partnership between you can join you together more as you plan your wedding as a shared vision.

So, as you go through this book, even though it's primarily you I am addressing, share the information with your partner. Give him the necessary details for the planning process, and allow him to share in the planning. There is no need to play superwoman, nor to adhere to an old-fashioned notion that the woman plans the wedding. Share the family dynamics section with him as well, so that you have a unified front when dealing with others. Remember, you are a team, and all plans now and forever are a team effort.

When one or both of you have children

If either you or your groom have children from a previous marriage, you're not just planning a wedding for the two of you, you're planning a wedding for *all* of you, and you are merging two families into one blended one. This is a very common situation now. Beth Reed Ramirez of *Bride Again, The Only Magazine for Encore Brides* reports that her recent survey shows that 64 percent of remarrying couples have children from previous marriages. That is a lot of blending families and a lot of family-oriented weddings.

Throughout this book, I provide ideas on how to incorporate your kids into every aspect of the wedding. Kids should be made to feel as if they're a special part of the day, a special part of the union. Some brides have their kids walk them down the aisle. Some kids perform music at their parents' ceremonies. Some do readings. Some serve as honor attendants. I will address not only the kids' involvement in the wedding itself, but also, in the Afterword, the issue of new family dynamics and family blending smarts. Family therapists have contributed to this section, as have real second-time brides who give advice from the real-life experience on how to handle kids' feelings, reactions, and needs.

Yes, this makes for something of a three-pronged effort—your wedding wishes, others' wedding wishes, and the kids' wedding wishes—but handled correctly, you can sail through the planning of the wedding and start your new family life in happiness and harmony.

Trends in second weddings

The great news for you is that the strict societal conventions regarding weddings are quickly evaporating. No longer are brides sticking to the dusty, old etiquette rules that say they can't wear white, they can't have a big wedding, and any other can'ts. Today's bride has so much more freedom in all wedding choices. The wedding industry has given its blessing to the second-time bride (because there are millions of you out there), and all options are much more diverse.

Weddings are not the cookie-cutter affairs they used to be, and brides are not having celebrations that have been carbon-copied from their mothers' era. There is a great deal of originality in second weddings. Some couples are having the large, elegant wedding they've always wanted. Some are running off to Hawaii to marry next to a waterfall. Some go on exotic adventure honeymoons. Some take their kids along on family vacations after the wedding. Second-time brides are wearing white. They're going barefoot on the beach. They're having honor attendants of the opposite gender. A great deal of originality is the norm rather than the exception now, so you are free to do away with tradition and plan whatever kind of wedding you desire.

Yes, there will always be detractors who will gossip about your choices, those dehydrated, bitter little crones who can tell you in which paragraph in the etiquette books your newest gaffe is listed. But the beauty of being a second-time bride is that you don't have to please everyone else. Let them complain. It's your wedding, and it's time to get started planning it right now.

Part One

The

Basics

Chapter 1

Wedding Planning Smarts

The wedding industry is a 32 billion-dollar conglomeration of many different types of businesses, with many different styles of service. As you plan your wedding, you will be walking into different worlds of artistry, service, rules and regulations, price ranges, and possibilities. With so many weddings taking place, with so much demand for the best in all wedding realms, the industry as a whole has its ups and downs in value.

You've heard stories of shady ring dealers, musicians who don't show up, and shriveled flower orders that look like they were put together two weeks before the wedding. These are just some of the dangers of an industry that has so much potential to be either really good or really bad. As in any profession, there are good and bad eggs in vendors and companies, and as you plan your wedding you will have to make sure you avoid all of the potentially harmful offerings out there.

I will not go so far as to say that some vendors are out to get clients who come in for consultations, but it is well known among wedding professionals that there are some crooks out there. To them, business is business, and they will take advantage where they can. One wedding vendor confided to me that it is standard practice in his type of company that when a young, innocent, naïve couple comes in to book an order, the sales associate bumps up the price. Some of these young couples have Daddy's gold card, the pros think, and some weddings mean anything goes.

Even if you do not present an image of being naïve or too-trusting, you may run across unscrupulous dealers who hype their service, offer substandard contracts at high prices, or otherwise manipulate you into a buy.

The wedding industry is an industry. Supply and demand is the rule, and certain vendors do know that they can take advantage when they smell an open-ended budget. They charm and flatter with "Hey, you should have the best because you're worth it," and they are quite evasive about the terms of their contract.

This isn't news to you. You've dealt with businesses before. You may not, however, have dealt with the wedding industry before. If you planned your own first wedding, you may not have been very focused on the business end of the details. Perhaps your parents took care of the signing, deposits, and contracts. Now, as a smarter, more competent and focused individual, you're going to get involved with an industry whose elements need to be handled just like any other smart business deal.

In this section, we'll handle the main ideas of smart wedding shopping, as these few guidelines can save you thousands of dollars and unnecessary headaches, disorganization, and stress.

Weddings and the Internet

The Internet has become a big part of the wedding industry. Just a few years ago, there was no such thing as online registry, wedding gown designers' Web sites, ordering gifts and favors off the Web, and posting your wedding pictures on your own homepage. While the Internet does provide you with a world of information, you should know that this information is only useful to you if you subject it to close scrutiny. Don't order items or gowns sight unseen. It may seem to be a smart savings of time, and a way of being organized, to plan your whole wedding over the Internet, but this causes new headaches. What are return policies? What are the true fees? Are these products I see on my screen really that great?

In the wedding industry, as in life, there is no replacement for the real thing. So use the Internet as a guide, gain your information, go ahead and register online, and subject all potential purchases to the same thinking as you would any other through a catalog or at a store. Allow plenty of time for returns and refunds, and keep careful track of your orders. Never order from a site that does not provide a secure connection for your personal information, and if a site asks for your password, pass it up. There are a lot of smaller, little known rip-off Web sites out there, and you don't want to get scammed on any aspect of your big day.

Smart wedding consumerism

You basically know this information from your previous wedding planning experiences, and from any other major event you've planned. But these elements are so important to your smart investment in your wedding that they must be outlined here.

Getting referrals

Before you hire any wedding professional in any realm of your wedding, ask newly married friends, friends who have recently planned special anniversary parties, bar/bat mitzvahs, retirement parties, and the like whom they would recommend. If you remember that your friend's wedding was awash with beautiful floral centerpieces, ask her whom she hired and if she would recommend them. Remember, just the appearance of those beautiful flowers does not mean that florist was a dream to work with. He may have been difficult about planning the order, late in delivery, and those centerpieces may not have been what your friend wanted. Ask to see if she would recommend them to you.

If you know no one with a connection to, say, a limousine company, call your local five-star hotel and ask the concierge for the name of the limousine company they hire to escort their biggest clients. Since the hotel stakes its reputation on the treatment and service of their contractors, they will most likely give you the names of the best in the business.

Recommendations and referrals must be sought from truly impartial subjects. Your photographer, as wonderful as he is, may recommend his friend the videographer whose work is just not that great. Use recommendations not as gospel, but as permission to put these choices on your interview list.

Comparison shopping

In any wedding area, whether it be florists, caterers, photographers, or gown shops, you will be best served by comparison shopping among all of your options. Too many brides book the first good thing that comes along, but haven't you learned that's not the right way to do things? Have a detailed list of questions and issues that you will use to compare and contrast all of your options, and use the answers on that list to decide which of the vendors is right for you.

The best comparison shoppers know that you cannot ask too many questions. If a manager is rude and impatient with your list of questions, then you have been given a sign that you will not receive the best treatment at that establishment. Good vendors know that concerned and informed brides are taking this event seriously, and they want to help create a lovely event for them. They also want the brides to recommend them to all of their sisters and college friends. The wedding industry is a word-of-mouth industry, and the best vendors know that you will refer them if you are happy with their treatment of you. In most instances, the comparison shopping segment of your planning process is going to help you weed out the unprofessional vendors to reveal the smaller crop of true finds.

Allow ample time to comparison shop. A rushed judgment is worthless. Make well-spaced appointments at each of your locations or companies, and ask for a sit-down interview. Here, you will ask all of your questions.

One of the most important things that vendors have shared with me is that just as it's important for the bride to get her details, the wedding pro has to have a long list of information from her. The pro needs to know the basic details of the wedding, such as size, formality, date, season, and style. Together, in a mutual partnership, the bride and a good vendor can discuss the realities of a business agreement and whether or not the pro can meet the bride's needs. You will be wasting your time if you can provide no solid information, so know what you want in general as you begin your search for the best professional in a field.

During your search for the best professional, you will be looking at samples of products, seeing if they meet your vision. Always request to see a real-life version of the item, not just a glossy picture in a catalog. You'll want to be sure the vendor's talent is true.

Get brochures and copies of ordering lists, price lists, and contracts as you do the comparison legwork. If managers balk about giving you a printed price list, consider what that means about their professionalism. Unless their industry is one that relys on ever-changing prices, such as the floral market, their standard packages should have printed prices applicable to all clients.

Checking contracts

You're smart. You're capable. You know that contracts are signed and sealed and enforceable in court. I know you won't make the same mistake that other brides have made in accepting verbal contracts, not checking the fine print, and forgetting to ask the big questions.

Basically, in any contract for any wedding services, from the florist to the reception site to the invitations, each contract should have all of the information needed for a complete recording of your agreement. Be sure your contracts have the following:

- The company's name.
- The company's address.
- The company's phone number.
- The company's e-mail.
- The name of the person you're contracting with.
- Your name, address, and phone number.
- The date of your wedding, including the day of the week (to prevent mix-ups).
- The location of your ceremony, including street address and phone number.
- The location of your reception, including street address and phone number.
- The complete, itemized list of what you're ordering (such as number of bouquets, specifying which kinds of flowers are to be used in them, numbers and styles of limousines, etc.).
- Delivery instructions and times to be delivered (this may take a separate order form).
- The complete price.
- Deposit amount and due date.
- Installment payment amounts and due dates.
- Refund policy and details of full refund.
- Cancellation policy and details of cancellation.

Another item to be included in any fair contract, where applicable, is the phrase "time is of the essence." According to Georgia attorney Karen Beyke, this phrase means that the vendor is bound to deliver the purchased items or services at a certain place by a certain time or the contract is null and void. For instance, take the case of Ellen. Her boutonnieres were not delivered to the church before the wedding and her men went without. The florist delivery man showed up 15 minutes into the wedding and stood at the back of the church with the box of men's flowers. A quick fix was had for the pictures and the reception, however, they weren't there for the original effect, and Ellen was not going to let that slide. After she returned from her honeymoon, she took her contract to the florist, pointed out the error, and received her partial refund stipulated by the "time is of the essence" clause.

As with any contract, you are free to make changes in the wording, if you initial your changes. If the wedding professional does not allow you to make changes to the contract, and your requests are within reason, find another professional. No contract should be that rigid, as you want to customize your wedding orders. Skip companies that do not allow your own choice for your own protection, and choose a company that looks out for your interests and is willing to allow you some freedom.

Be pleasant to deal with

I'm not asking you to be a wispy-breath doormat, or to acquiesce to every demand of the vendor. In fact, I'm asking quite the opposite. You'll find that you can get your way, stand up for your rights, and gain quality results with a pleasant demeanor much more easily than with a crack-the-whip "I am the customer, and the customer is always right!" attitude. Wedding professionals love to deal with brides who are smart, know what they want, are respectful of their time, and know how to ask for changes.

All it takes is a little diplomacy, an air of confidence, and a dose of fairness to make you the dream customer, and wedding pros do more for dream customers. If you begin your relationship with a wedding professional—and it *is* a relationship—as a pushy, demanding, never-satisfied, whining, ambivalent, or mean person with no regard for the pro's humanity, you will not receive much more than your own attitude in return.

So be organized, be kind, *say thank you* (a common complaint in the industry), and express your feelings and wishes directly rather than having the professional guess or labor under a false sense of vision.

Be organized

Keep all of your wedding planning materials in one place. Use a calendar so you have recordings of when deposits were paid, when they are due, and when fittings and pickups will be. Disorganized brides waste time and money, and they do not endear themselves to others when their disorganization infringes on others' time.

You may not have the patience or the personality to create a file folder system or use a computer CD-ROM to keep everything in line, but you should use your own best organizational system to stay on top of all the details. One bride suggested having one fat spiral notebook by the phone for all wedding notes, for the recording of all important calls made, for the recording of all important phone and cell phone numbers. Keeping every-thing together saves you headaches that have been suffered by other brides who just did not keep their receipts and contracts together.

Some online wedding sites do provide highly organized programs for keeping track of guest responses, your budget, and your registry. Use these free offerings, but be sure to print out your information on a regular basis. If the site "blinks" or loses your information, you're organized system is out the window, and you will certainly panic. I would. So keep technology's limitations in mind if you're going the online route for organization.

Confirm everything

You already know this from your first wedding, but it bears repeating. *All* orders and bookings need to be confirmed several times before the big day. You don't have to call every day. That would be excessive. Just call three weeks ahead of time, then one week ahead of time, then two days before. That's all you need to do. Any potential problems, forgotten orders (it happens) or last-minute payment problems can be dealt with in a non-crisis atmosphere, and you have the peace of mind of knowing that all of your details are well-in-hand, and that your vendors are all set.

Hiring a wedding consultant

You're a busy person, and you may not have time for all the running around, interviewing, sampling, and booking. In this case, as many brides do, you might want to hire a wedding consultant to take care of the planning.

This is a highly individual decision, as you may not want to give up con-trol of this wedding too. While time constraints may encourage you to leave it all up to a professional and trust her ability to create your vision, do you really want a second "mom" making all the calls, no matter how talented and well-connected she is?

On the other hand, the best wedding coordinators can plan a wedding exactly to your specifications, and you may find that it's the end result that matters most. You simply may not have time to spend doing all the plan-ning, and you may be fine with hiring the best consultant around. You may have the budget for it as well.

Many brides are attracted to this option, but they worry about the cost of it. I spoke to Shirley Feuerstein of Affairs and Arrangements about that very issue, and she walked me through the process:

Coordinators' packages

First of all, wedding coordinators have involvement packages now. No longer do they just swoop in and take over the whole thing. Knowing the position of brides, those with busy lives but minds and wishes of their own, the best consultants offer full package services that include the handling of every aspect down to the design of the forks and knives, partial packages for the bride's selection of the best wedding vendors, and wedding day packages during which the coordinator just shows up to run the day. Overall, coordinators in the wedding industry have tailored their offerings to match the needs of the modern-day bride, and one of these options may be attractive to you.

Finding the best coordinator

Wedding coordinators are listed in the phone book, but you should do more than just choose the one with the nicest ad. Because a coordinator does play a crucial role in the creation of a wedding, you will have to be sure to interview your candidates well:

- Is she a member of the Association of Bridal Consultants?
- Is she a member of the International Special Events Society?
- What kinds of packages does she offer?
- How are her prices in relation to the services she will provide?
- Does she ask for a flat fee or a percentage of the wedding costs? Never hire someone who works on commission, as she is not looking out for the bride's best interest. If, for instance, she hires a more expensive band, she gets more of the cut out of your pocketbook.
- Does she offer a free first consultation?
- Does she have pictures or video of other events that she has planned?
- Does she have high profile clients in the area?
- Does she handle your kind of wedding (outdoor, location, etc.)?
- Does she listen to you, or is she just talking? Some consultants have bossy personalities, and you would be best served in assessing her for her personality style. After all, you will be in a working relationship for a long time. Is she someone you want to work with?
- How many weddings is she handling that week?
- Does she have a limit as to how many weddings or events she'll do in a week? (The best do set limits.)
- Does she hire assistants to help out at the wedding?

❧ Are these assistants trained? You may not know it, but the ideal assistant is an apprentice in the wedding/event planning industry and not just some high school kids who want to make $12 an hour. Some brides report frustration at the coordinator's young assistants who did more mingling at the wedding than serving and helping out.

Overall, the best indication is how the coordinator makes you feel. She doesn't have to go over the top, trying to flatter you into booking every service she has, but she should be a comfortable person to be with. She should be willing to talk about your ideas, talk about what you don't want, show you samples, and respect you as a client. Remember, she too wants you to recommend her to your friends, but she also wants to do a great job on your wedding. I've found that coordinators are attracted to their job because they love to create. They love to make people happy. They love to get all the details just right. Finding the right coordinator means finding another helpful partner in the creation of your day.

Bridal industry pitfalls

With enough advance planning time, you can avoid most industry pit-falls. It is mostly the bride who is planning an enormous wedding in a short amount of time who stumbles into difficult planning situations. Still, you may encounter some of these problems, so be wary, and make smart decisions at all times.

Avoid:

❧ Booking the first thing you see. It won't save you time. It will just prevent you from finding a better offer.

❧ Being desperate. Coming right out and saying, "I don't care what it costs, I'll pay anything" for that gorgeous gown/cake/floral display, is the mark of a first-timer. So be clear about what your budget is, and do not allow yourself to be talked into spending more because "you're worth it."

❧ Taking a "too good to be true" offer. Usually, these one-time-only advertisements for ring sales and gown clearances can present frauds and fakes. Research fully, and be careful of fool's gold offers.

❧ Not getting a contract. You know better than this.

* Paying in cash. All purchases should be done on a credit card so that your company can either stop payment, refund you, or report fraud. True, some credit card companies are not running at 100% in the refund department right now, but at least you'll have a record of the sale on your statement. A cash transaction can be disputed.

Make sure to:

* Only work with established businesses that have had years of experience. I always tell brides to shop at stores that have been around for a long time, not the fly-by-night jeweler that just popped up last week and could be gone next week.
* Take no shortcuts. Measure areas for dance floors, measure tables, measure doorways for adequate space and the delivery of items.
* Get all deliveries via certified, return-receipt mail. Send all packages, such as your maids' gowns, the same way.
* Take a look at everything. Don't book a boat you haven't seen, don't book rentals you haven't seen. You don't want any unpleasant surprises on the wedding day.
* Stand your ground. Don't be talked into—or out of—anything without your full understanding.
* Don't plan when you're too stressed. Realize your limits and change an appointment if you have to, rather than make decisions out of frustration or impatience.
* Remember to enjoy the process. Keep a wedding journal to record all of the *good* parts about planning the wedding. Too often, brides just record the appointments, the problems, the questions. Use your journal or notebook to write down the touching, funny, silly, or memorable moments. After the chaos of the planning process is done, you'll have this memento to remember that it wasn't that difficult. The bad stuff may be louder, but the good stuff is forever if you record it that way.

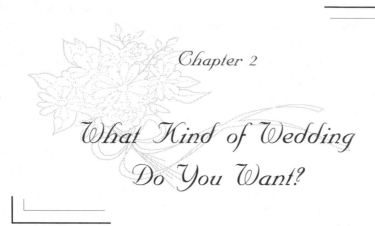

Chapter 2

What Kind of Wedding Do You Want?

Before you can make any decisions, any purchases, or take on the wedding industry, you'll need to have a very clear idea of exactly what kind of wedding you want. You'll need to have every detail planned out according to your own vision, so that you will be able to make smart decisions and create the celebration you desire. It is not enough to say, "I want a big wedding with all the trimmings" or "I want a small, intimate wedding with just our closest friends and family." You'll need to be able to differentiate between a garden wedding and all that entails and a traditional wedding with every etiquette strand in place. In this section, you will create your picture of the kind of wedding you want, taking into account that your vision will depend on a few outside factors: your budget, your style and tastes, what the groom wants, and yes, the fact that this time it's all within your control. You're not having your mother's wedding. It's all yours, and the creative freedom is yours as well. So use this chapter to set the foundation for the wedding you've both always wanted, and let the fun begin.

Defining your second dream wedding

Ask yourself some questions first. How do you picture your wedding? Is it a traditional one in a church, with a lavish reception at a banquet hall? Is it an improved version of your first wedding? Or is it an informal wedding in a garden, with bright sunflowers all around and your flower girls dancing barefoot on the lawn with floral wreaths in their hair?

Do you see yourself on a beach, with the surf gently rolling in the background, the sun on your shoulders, and a beautiful seafood buffet as the reception dinner?

Perhaps your vision is more tropical. Will you exchange vows in a Hawaiian rainforest, wearing fragrant leis around your necks, surrounded by the deep greens and vibrant colors of exotic flowers and a roaring waterfall behind you?

Or do you see an outdoor wedding in your backyard with an enormous white tent strung with little white lights, a strolling violinist, a butler passing hors d'oeuvres, and floral arrangements on every level surface?

No doubt, you've thought about the vision of your wedding ever since your fiancé popped the question—and maybe beforehand—so now it's time to focus on the type of wedding you *are* going to have. You'll eliminate the other options, narrow in on all of the details of your particular celebration, and plan according to what you want.

The wonderful news is that you have a great deal of freedom. The first-time bride is more constrained by traditional etiquette and others' wishes, and she doesn't always get the wedding of her dreams. Your wedding, on the other hand, is less bound by tradition and etiquette, and today's wedding industry understands that. You will not hear "No, you can't do that" from any wedding professional, and you'll ignore anyone else who tries to force an etiquette book into your hand. You'll undoubtedly have strong feelings about doing your wedding your way this time, and you do have the freedom to do that.

Learning from your first wedding

As mentioned earlier, you are no doubt looking back at your first wedding, sometimes with sentimentality and sometimes with regret. That's reality. You may be quite sad that you will not be able to have the big-splash wedding that you had the first time, due to financial constraints, and you may be bitter that you wasted that first wedding planning process on someone you never should have married. Or, you may be wistful when trying on wedding gowns again if your previous spouse passed away. Whatever your situation, you have been the bride before, and you're walking through the wedding realm as a second-timer.

The best frame of mind to keep is that your first wedding was important in its time. It was what it was, and you were most likely happy with it then. Now, you have the chance to see it as a model, not as the milestone it was then. Now, you can look at each part of it objectively and decide which elements you liked and which you'd rather do differently.

Perhaps you want the entire wedding to be completely different. Perhaps you're the emotional type, and you don't want one thing about this wedding to remind you of your first. "It was important to me to have everything as different as possible," says Nancy, a second-time bride. "Not because I hated my ex and hated thinking about my first wedding—that wasn't the case—but because that wedding had so few elements of my own in it. Everything was either what my mother wanted, what my father wanted, what my ex's mother wanted, even what he wanted. Very little of it was my dream, although on that day I thought it was. Looking back now, I know exactly what I want and what I don't want this time."

Every encore bride has her own reasons for wanting things to be either similar to or different from her first wedding. Some pull out their old wedding planners or folders—if they still have them—and looked at what actually went into the planning of the first wedding, where they made their decisions. Many thought about what the financial control situation meant to their decision-making power. That's a universal issue with second-time brides. Most likely, your parents are not paying for this wedding, so the decisions are up to you. And you're not likely to plan the same wedding your parents planned for you.

So think back now over your first wedding.

What did you love? The flowers? Your gown? Having a big bridal party? Having a big guest list?

What would you do differently? Have a DJ instead of a band? Have fewer guests, with more of them being your friends than your parents'? Have a smaller bridal party? Have a wider range of menu options for the reception? Play different music?

It's important to handle this step now, at one shot and right in the beginning of the process. Otherwise, any deep-seated reminders of your first wedding might pop up and hit you in an emotional way as you're making your wedding plans. Some brides find that planning a second wedding raises some old issues that need to be dealt with. Hopefully, you've dealt with the end of your first marriage fully, to the point of being ready to marry again, but it is unavoidable that planning a second wedding will remind you of your first. So make peace with it now, remind yourself that this time is for real and that you will have the wedding you want.

Most second-time brides I spoke to said the wedding planning process this time around was far more enjoyable than the first, and that the decisions made were easier this time due to the absence of pressure and constraints. Although they did think about their first weddings, they thought about them differently. The first wedding was a fantasy affair, the big day, a starry-eyed production. This wedding, in contrast, is more about the meaning of the day. It's a celebration, but that starry-eyed thing is not there. Sure, there is joy and euphoria, overwhelming happiness, but the focus is on creating a day that speaks of the partnership between you and your groom. All of the elements are personalized, not taken out of a magazine or florist's book, and once that realization is made, it is easy to analyze the first wedding for the pieces that worked and the pieces that didn't.

Why am I even addressing this? Isn't it a bad move to remind you of a wedding that's connected to a marriage that didn't work? I do it because it's necessary, because I don't want to see you make hasty decisions out of superstition or bitterness. I don't want you to try to make everything so different this time around that you disappoint yourself. Your first wedding was just an event, and you can use some of the elements from it in this wedding.

What does the groom want?

Again, if this is the groom's first wedding, he may want to have the grand affair for his own experience. And you may not fight him much on that. Or this may be his second wedding too, and he may share your feelings that you may both have been through this before, but this time it's more special.

At this early step of the planning process, it's important to sit down with your fiancé and discuss what he wants for your wedding. He may just shrug and say "It's your day," or he may have strong feelings about having another ultra-formal affair. All cases will be different. Still, his input is important in this wedding, as you will be working as a team. It's not you and your mother making all the plans, it's the two of you. So he should get some input on the plans, even if it's just a few yes's or no's.

I don't have to tell you that your groom is unlikely to want to make the wedding planning a very big deal in his life. He may be willing to spend an hour or two looking at sample books or calling around for prices. Just ask him outright what level of involvement he wants. He will respect you for considering his wishes, his time, and his ability level on these matters, and he will be a more willing partner if you're not pressuring him to help you.

Assessing your budget

As mentioned earlier, your budget is going to be a big factor when deciding the wedding you'll be able to plan. Again, you may not have your parents paying for the whole thing, so there is no golden checkbook. The expenses are up to the two of you, and it's up to you to make the most of your wedding budget money.

The first step is deciding how much you have to spend on the wedding. Taking your prior financial responsibilities into consideration—loans, car payments, insurance, college education for the kids, alimony payments—assessing your wedding budget from what's left over may be a sobering task. Many couples sit down for the all-important Money Talk and find that the wedding of their dreams may just have to remain a dream unless they win the lottery.

However, you may not find yourself in that situation. Most second-time brides and grooms are older and established in their careers, with solid credit and some money set aside over the years. In fact, industry experts say their second-time clients have more money to spend on their weddings, as they do have a more independent and stronger financial background.

Whichever camp you belong to, whether or not you have a big financial reserve for this wedding, you'll still make all of your decisions based on what kinds of funds you have available. Everything from the flowers to the limos to the marriage license takes money, and it will take good budgeting for you to get the most out of each wedding category with what you have to spend.

What are other second-time brides spending?

Well, all weddings are different, and all financial levels are different all over the country. Second-time brides may choose smaller, more intimate weddings, or they may go for the big bash. Nationally, the averages of budgets are higher than you might expect, which shows that many second-time couples are pulling out all the stops for their celebrations.

According to a survey done recently by *Bride Again* magazine, here are the average amounts spent in the biggest budget categories by second- and third-time brides:

The Wedding Gown:		Wedding Rings:	
Up to $999	10%	Up to $1,999	12%
$1,000 to 1,999	26%	$2,000 to 2,499	15%
$2,000 to 2,999	47%	$2,500 to 3,999	34%
$3,000 to 3,999	11%	$4,000 to 4,999	28%
Over $4,000	6%	Over $5,000	11%

Reception:		Honeymoons:	
Under $1,999	8%	Under $1,999	14%
$2,000 to 3,499	11%	$2,000 to 2,999	21%
$3,500 to 4,999	23%	$3,000 to 3,999	17%
$5,000 to 6,499	37%	$4,000 to 4,999	25%
$6,500 to 7,999	10%	$5,000 to 7,499	18%
$8,000 to 9,999	5%	$7,500 to 9,999	3%
Over $10,000	6%	Over $10,000	2%

Total Wedding Costs:	
Under $3,999	14%
$4,000 to $6,999	26%
$7,000 to $12,999	31%
$13,000 to $24,999	24%
Over $25,000	5%

Remember, those are national averages, taking into account everything from a country-style wedding to a posh New York City affair. I supply them here so that you can be reminded that you are free to spend a fair amount of money on the wedding of your dreams, provided you spend it well and do not get yourself into irreversible debt to finance your day.

Prioritizing your budget

This time, you get to decide where the money is going to go. Do you want to put the bulk of your available budget into the reception? Into the honeymoon? Into a Vera Wang gown? You may not be able to break the budget up into an exact pie chart, but you should decide now which elements of your wedding are most important to you and which you'll want to spend the most on.

Setting your budget

Once you've assessed your available funds, accepted any contributions from family members (your parents may still want to kick in as a gift to you), and prioritized where the money will be allocated, it's time to make up your master budget.

I know, sticking to a budget is difficult, and you may not want to be constrained by a number on a piece of paper when you see a fabulous cake that you just have to have. But trust me, a written budget—even one that's not set in stone—will keep your spending in line and keep you somewhat on the path of your allowable funds. Shopping without a budget can lead to impulse ordering, conflicts with your fiancé, and greater financial constraints with later purchases.

In Appendix D, you'll find a worksheet where you'll record your estimated and actual expenses. Use this tool to keep a handle on your budget.

Size does matter

Your budget is going to dictate not only what kind of gown you can get, or the range of appetizers at your cocktail hour, but how many guests you can invite.

There is no blanket rule that states that a big wedding is always going to be more expensive than a small wedding. Indeed, an informal big wedding can cost less than an ultra-formal small wedding with all of the five-star treatment a celebrity might order. All of your decisions at this early stage do work together. From your budget, to the size, to the style of the wedding, the elements that you're dealing with will dictate the wedding you have.

Taking into consideration whether you want an informal outdoor wedding with 100 guests, or a wedding on a yacht with 75 guests, or a formal wedding with 50 guests—and then factoring in other elements—you will have to make up your guest list to help you make the next decisions down the line.

The two of you should start by drawing up your combined guest list, and then each of you should add the names of your friends, colleagues, clients, and other special people in your lives. This time around, the guest list is yours. Close family may be invited, but this time your parents will just show up. Second-time weddings are far more enjoyable, say most brides, because they include the people in the bride's and groom's lives. It's your crowd, no one else's. (If you have children, you might allow them to bring guests for their own comfort.)

If you are on good terms with your ex, you may choose to invite him as well. Many brides say that this was a good move, provided they really are on good terms with their exes. The kids will see that their mom and dad still support each other, and that your ex supports your new marriage. This may cut down on future power struggles and any uncomfortable feelings of split loyalty on the kids' part. This one is completely up to you. Are you on truly good terms with your ex? What if he brings his girlfriend, the one he left you for? And what of your fiancé's side of this decision? What if he invites his ex-wife? How will you feel about her simmering over in the corner? Obviously, this is something the two of you must discuss.

All weddings have their share of guest list woes, people who are bitter about the marriage, various detractors, volatile undercurrents. The main issue is that you are in charge. You should invite only your closest loved ones and make the decisions for yourselves. Do not invite your ex if you don't trust him to behave himself. Only a truly established level of comfort will do here.

"For this wedding, I knew I wanted all of my closest friends and cousins to be invited. At my first wedding, there was only room on the guest list for five of my friends—I was young and didn't speak up—and I lost some good friends who were insulted that they weren't invited. Now, I get to have who I want there, and it's so much better."

—Tracy

"We didn't want a big wedding. We wanted a more elegant wedding for fewer people, so that we could have the finest food, the finest champagne, the finest desserts at a lovely small room in the best reception facility in the state. Our intimate reception was so memorable, people talked about it for years. It was the wedding of my dreams, because it was simple and elegant....like we are."

—Morgan

A formal affair?

As you well know, level of formality is also one of the defining aspects of the wedding you'll be planning. The formality of your wedding will determine the wardrobe of all involved, the menu, the décor, even the location. If you have a formal event in mind, you know that's the traditional wedding of standard fare, where the men wear tuxes and the women wear gowns.

Things have not changed too much in the wedding industry regarding formality, but you should be reminded of the rules so that you can tell your wedding vendors and professionals the category of wedding you'll be planning. They'll need to know, for example, if it's a formal outdoor, an informal indoor, an informal beach, or a formal yacht wedding. Here are the descriptions of each:

Formal:

Women wear floor-length gowns or cocktail length dresses.
Men wear black tuxedoes and black ties.
Event is sit-down dinner or elegant buffet.

Semi-formal:

Women wear floor-length or the more popular cocktail-length dresses.
Men wear dark formal suits or dark dinner jackets.
Catering is either light or full buffet, or a sit-down dinner.

Informal:

Women wear dresses of the same make, color, and length as the bride's gown.
Men wear suits to match the season, and to match each other.

You may already know all of this, but it is important that you be able to explain the formality of the wedding to every professional on your list. All of the decisions do connect to make a unified wedding statement, and it's the best way to communicate suitable ideas.

Chapter 3

Setting the Date

Now that you've had a good look at your available budget, you can judge when you want the wedding to be held. A wedding date set for a year from now will give you more time to save extra money. Your ability to wait will mean that you can afford more of the extras or put more cash into the elements of your wedding.

If you're not in a position where you'd like to wait a while in order to save some extra cash, then you can look for suitable dates at any time that's good for you. Your budget is all set, you know what you want, and it's time to set the date that will be written in that lovely print on your invitations.

Choosing a season for the wedding

You may know that the most popular months for weddings are June, July, and September, but May and October are gaining in popularity. With these being the high wedding months, they are also the time that most sites and services will already be booked, or will be more expensive due to supply and demand.

June wedding dates are usually the first to be booked up, as many brides want to go for that traditional June bride sentimentality. But the early fall is becoming more of a choice time, as the colorings of natural surroundings lend themselves well to outdoor photos.

As far as popularity, and the resulting spike in prices, Valentine's Day, New Year's Eve, and the Fourth of July have long been a choice of brides who want to hold their weddings on meaningful, celebratory days. While these days may mean higher prices for flowers, champagne, and the like, they are also a wonderful way to mark the beginning of your marriage. Valentine's Day, the most romantic day of the year, is a top pick for obvious reasons. New Year's Eve means a big party and an extra celebration at midnight, the striking of the clock signaling a new beginning. The Fourth of July may mean a free fireworks backdrop for your reception, if you plan well.

You know the seasons you love. You may be a fall person. You may love the colors, the scent in the air, the changing of the leaves, the crisp mornings and warm afternoons. These are the times to look at when planning the wedding in your mind's eye.

For bigger discounts, all wedding professionals say that they drop their prices in the "off" months: January, February, and November. The wedding industry goes by the concept of in-season and out-of-season. That goes for everything from gowns to flowers to foods, and also for the entire industry itself. You'll be quite familiar with this concept by the time you finish this book, as we will discuss it a lot. For now, think about which month and season is "in season" for you.

The day of the week

Although Saturday weddings are still the most popular, Friday night weddings are making their way into the headlines of the wedding world. Friday weddings have several advantages, the first of which is that they are less expensive. Hotels and banquet halls are seeing this opportunity as a way to get another event into the weekend, and they offer their standard packages for less on a Friday night. This might mean travel difficulties for your guests, but your wedding will be every bit as beautiful on a Friday as it will on a Saturday. Another benefit is that you may get lower airfare if you can leave the next day for your honeymoon.

Sundays too are good choices for a wedding, particularly if your guests are all from nearby locations. Depending upon your ceremony site, you may have to have an afternoon wedding, but many brides report having Sunday morning weddings in a non-religious setting followed by an enormous Sunday brunch. The prices for this option are lower, as a Sunday wedding event is not the norm.

For extremely small and less formal weddings, we're now seeing Thursday night celebrations. For instance, some brides are booking a small meeting room or banquet room in a hotel, holding their ceremony there with either a religious leader, a mayor, or a Justice of the Peace, and then having their receptions in that room or in a nearby jazz lounge or restaurant.

The date you pick does depend on the rest of the details of your wedding, but there are more options than just Saturday open to you.

Which dates work for you?

Of course, you're going to need to check which dates work for you. Perhaps you are in the middle of law school, or you won't have enough vacation days saved up until next year. Is this the busy season at work? Are your kids in school? When will they be on vacation?

It goes without saying that you need to be able to attend your own wedding, but it's best to look ahead now at what may be going on in your life during the time you're looking at for the big event. You may need to talk to your boss about needing time off for the wedding and honeymoon. You may need to do extra work ahead of time to make up for your absence.

As for your kids, you need to look at their schedules to see what days they have off, and what activities they have planned for that time. Your teenage daughter, for instance, will hate you if you plan your wedding for the day of the big homecoming dance or her prom. Your son may have a hockey playoff game that night, and he won't want to miss it. So avoid potential scheduling nightmares by planning well for you and for your family right now.

Can others make it?

One of the most important parts of a wedding is having your closest loved ones there to share the moment with you. So if you want all of your friends and relatives to be at the celebration, you'd best take some time now to consider their schedules if you consider them a vital part of the day, especially if they'll be in your bridal party.

Although it is asking a bit much for you to plan your schedule around finding a weekend that's free for 50 people, you should look at the bigger issues in your closest loved ones' lives:

- Are they still in college?
- Will they be in finals then?
- Are they in law school or medical school, preparing for the bar or their boards?
- Are they pregnant? When are they due?
- Is there an illness the person is facing? Surgery? Chemotherapy?
- Will they be traveling for special work-related events?
- Is that their family vacation time?
- Do they already have a family vacation booked?
- Will the kids be on vacation from school then, or will they have to be pulled out to attend your wedding?
- Is that a big time of year for graduations or other special events?

Think about your loved ones' schedules, call around or e-mail to see which dates are out of the question. Your closest friends will love it that you think enough of them to consider their time constraints, and that you truly want them at your wedding. Of course, you will not be able to please everyone, but you can make your best efforts.

Considering Mother Nature

Even if your wedding will not be held outdoors, the weather will still be a factor. There is, of course, no way to predict a stormy weekend months ahead of time, but you can follow the natural patterns of your location for the rainiest or snowiest times of the year.

Remember that the stormy season produces travel delays and hazards, and perhaps power outages in your area. The hottest time of year is not the time for an outdoor wedding no matter how many fans you have. Your guests will swelter, the cake will melt off the table, and fainting is a definite possibility. So do think ahead to the weather of the particular time of year you're proposing as your wedding date, and plan accordingly.

Some brides and grooms go as far as to think about the weather where they want to go on their honeymoon. It may be cold in March on the East Coast, but it's fabulous in the islands. So they plan their weddings to meet the perfect air and water temperature on vacation for two weeks afterward!

Whatever your plans, be sure that Mother Nature is more likely than not to comply with your wishes.

Dates to avoid:

- Tax week in April.
- Friday the 13th, unless you're not superstitious.
- The date of your first wedding, for obvious reasons.
- The anniversary date of a family tragedy.
- Any date near one of your children's birthdays. Let them have their own celebration weekend.
- Memorial Day or Labor Day weekend. The travel hassles may be just too difficult for your guests.
- The dates you turn the clock back in the fall or forward in the spring. Too many people show up at the wrong time.

Great dates to consider:

- The anniversary of the date you met.
- Valentine's Day.
- New Year's Eve.
- Fourth of July.
- The anniversary of your engagement.
- Spring or Summer Solstice. For some, this is a new beginning.

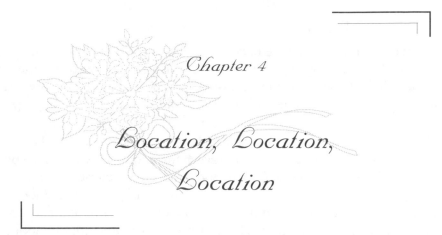

Chapter 4

Location, Location, Location

You've got the who, what, when, and how much. Now it's time to figure out the where. As a second-time bride, your options are far more open than those of a first-time bride. Most of those first-timers find themselves bound by tradition and family expectations, with no option other than having the ceremony at a church and the reception at a lavish reception hall. Sure, some venture into other settings, but not to the degree that second-time brides do.

According to Beth Reed Ramirez, editor of *Bride Again*, only 36 percent of second-time brides are doing the traditional chapel wedding, with a growing 58 percent choosing an outdoor or destination wedding. You second-timers, then, are looking for more individual locations, sites of beauty, and breaks with tradition. Many of these weddings, says Ramirez, at 38 percent, are outdoor events.

A growing number of couples are also choosing to hold their ceremonies and receptions at the same place. If the traditional church or synagogue wedding is not for you, you may opt to have the ceremony at one part of your site, and then head over to the tent for the reception portion. This option is an attractive one for most encore-wedding couples, as they do not have to concern themselves with transportation between the two places, extra site fees, extra permits, and directions for guests.

Although this may be the choice for you, I will still offer information on choosing a ceremony site and a reception site. The questions vary for each, so be sure to pay attention to all of the questions and criteria for any site you're considering.

Choosing a ceremony site

For you, it may be a simple decision. You wouldn't dream of marrying anywhere else but your longtime church or synagogue. You've counseled with the officiant, provided the necessary paperwork, and taken any necessary courses, and your church is available on the day you'd like. Simple, done.

But it may not be that easy. You may not belong to a particular religious institution, and you may have to search for a house of worship of your faith that will take you. Some brides report that they experienced a lot of trouble with this task, as some priests refused to marry non-parishioners. Some brides have confided that the priest at hand did not think the couple should be getting married again in his church. So they went door to door to different churches, looking for one that would accept them for marriage rites.

If you are planning a wedding in an official house of worship, ask these questions:

Questions to ask about a house of worship:

- Is it available on that day?
- At what time?
- Does that time match the formality of your wedding?
- Are there any other weddings planned for that site on that day?
- At what time?
- Is there enough time in between that ceremony and yours?
- Is the site large enough to accommodate all of your guests?
- Is there handicapped access for your special-needs guests?
- Is there air conditioning or heat, depending upon the season?
- Are there restrooms available to your guests?
- Is the site attractive?
- Is there a site fee?
- An officiant's fee?
- An organist's fee?
- What classes are required?
- What documentation is required?
- What are the officiant's list of rules about what can and can't be included in the ceremony?

This last one is very important, as many brides and grooms have discovered—too late—that their officiant does not allow flash photography or recording in the church. Such an officiant may also want approval of all songs, readings, speeches, and vows before he will agree to perform the ceremony. Be sure, when you're investigating religious ceremony sites, that any potential rigid rules do not affect your plans.

Ceremony site alternatives

As mentioned earlier, 38 percent of second-time couples are choosing to have outdoor ceremonies. That may mean a backyard service, complete with rows of rented white chairs, a trellis or bridal arch, and a portable podium or altar for the exchange of vows. I'll write more about outdoor weddings later in this chapter. For now, I want to suggest some other wonderful locations that brides have chosen for their unique and personalized weddings.

According to Diane Forden, editor-in-chief of *Bridal Guide*, the most popular sites for second-time weddings are bed-and-breakfasts, mansions, and yachts.

The bed-and-breakfast offers a charming backdrop to a wedding, often with a Victorian touch, one or several large fireplaces, décor straight from the pages of a magazine layout, a wraparound porch, and perhaps a yard with a lovely landscape. The bridal couple can book the best room in the house and enjoy a sumptuous breakfast brought to their bedside the next morning. To find a bed-and-breakfast in your area, check the local tourism board or ask your travel agent for the highest rated B & B nearby. Several bed-and-breakfast guidebooks and Web sites exist, but a more localized search will turn up the best results for you.

Mansions or historical estates are among the most beautiful and unique choices for wedding sites. Very often, the house is ornate, with gilded accents, Victorian décor, elegant lighting, and sweeping staircases. The home may have a lovely sunroom or porch and beautifully landscaped grounds with gardens or fountains. As it is such a major departure from the usual wedding site, the commonly decorated church, and the standard reception hall, guests are enthralled with the environment, often wandering around to explore rooms and marvel at the scenery.

Several wedding professionals I spoke to said they highly enjoyed creating weddings at these sites due to their natural beauty and the auras of the homes. These houses have long histories and personalities of their own, and the bridal couple will become a part of it. To find a historical home or estate that is open for public rental or use, contact your local historical society.

Yachts. From the enormous enclosed party yachts to a smaller, privately owned yacht that holds 12, weddings afloat can be a wonderful choice. A qualified officiant will marry you on deck as the sun sets over the horizon and the lights of the city form your backdrop. So many couples love the idea of "sailing off into the sunset," choosing this romantic and private option, that a great deal of wedding cruise options have arisen in the industry. Check with your local travel agent for the best wedding cruises in your area, or thoroughly research privately owned yachts for rent with a crew.

Weekend-long getaways are also popular now for second-time weddings. Couples are choosing to have not only the 15-minute ceremony and the four-hour reception, but also a full weekend of activities and time shared. Couples who have chosen this option say that a weekend outing to the beach or the mountains brings the family together. Planned tours, fun family competitions, cookouts, fancy dinners at four-star gourmet restaurants, and horseback riding on the beach are just some of the ideas these brides have had for their weekend weddings. The time spent together leads to bonding of the entire extended family, and this vacation-type atmosphere is far more relaxing than one emotionally intense day. So think about which kind of weekend getaway you want: a beach weekend, a ski weekend, or a grand touristy romp through the nearest major city, and book your plans for three days of activity...plus your wedding.

A beach wedding is also a lovely idea, one shared by many celebrities and couples who have an affinity for all things seaside. Beachside weddings are usually very informal, with the bride in a slipdress and perhaps bare feet, and the guests dressed up in informal clothing. Booking a site for a beach wedding depends upon the rules of your region. Most private and public beaches do require you to get a permit for a public gathering, cooking, or alcohol consumption, so find out from your town hall about the realities of this option for you.

An arboretum is a popular choice among brides right now. With its natural beauty and flawless design, the smell of the blooms, the arrangements of greenery, the fountains, and the butterflies, it's a piece of Eden. No wonder so many brides book their weddings in arboretums or botanical gardens. There they can be surrounded by English or tropical gardens without paying a penny to the florist.

Other site choices include scenic parks, lighthouses, museums, art galleries, country clubs, restaurant decks overlooking a calm lake, a clearing in a forest, or a specially booked site at an amusement park, casino, or hotel.

Of course, you might go the simple route as far as your ceremony goes and book some time with a Justice of the Peace or a judge. Attorney Karen Beyke of Marietta, Georgia says that most judges of the magistrate, state, or superior courts do perform wedding ceremonies. Some will even come to your venue for an extra fee. "Usually, you'll have to give them about two months' lead time in order for them to fit you into their schedules," says Beyke. Still, most couples married by judges choose to exchange vows in a no-nonsense ceremony at the courthouse. Afterwards, the reception can begin.

The outdoor wedding

Because the outdoor wedding is primarily a combined site for the ceremony and reception, I'll tackle the main site issues here.

An outdoor wedding may be beautiful, the stuff of dreams and all the rage now in the wedding industry, but it is not more simple or less expensive than a standard, traditional wedding in a banquet hall. In fact, it may be twice the work. Not only do you have to rent a tent, tables, chairs, dance floors, and most other items and hire on-site wedding professionals who must assess your outdoor location for adequate power supplies, light, and level ground, but you will also have to deal with the weather.

You've already read about Mother Nature's tendency to "crash" weddings, but nowhere is her influence felt more strongly than in the planning of an outdoor wedding. Most brides think that their tent will save the day in case of rain, but they do not realize that some rainstorms can cause power outages and unsafe conditions such as lightning and flooding. Many couples have had to evacuate their guests to another location, such as inside the house, crowding one hundred people into the family living and dining room as the bride sobs in her bedroom.

Event coordinator Shirley Feuerstein of Affairs and Arrangements suggests putting forth the effort to make a detailed backup plan in case the weather interferes with your outdoor wedding. Have a second location ready to go, even if that means you've spent the morning making extra room in your house in case of crowds. Most weddings are not subject to rain dates, so you will have to decide what will happen in case of a weather interruption.

Who will watch The Weather Channel to see if it's just a passing shower? Who will get generators to keep the power going in case of a neighborhood-wide blackout? These pre-planned steps have to be addressed, so that your outdoor wedding can come off without a hitch.

While the outdoor wedding may seem like a burden to plan, with its double-pronged approach, there is nothing more beautiful than a wedding of this sort. Event planners and brides and grooms rave about the outdoor celebrations they've held, saying that their pictures came out divine, their guests mingled more freely, and birds and butterflies fluttered around the outskirts of the party. "All that was missing was the rainbow," says one bride. And if it does shower briefly before your wedding, you may get one of those as well.

Choosing a reception location

Whether your reception will be held in a traditional reception hall, in an estate home, on a boat, or in your backyard, you'll have to asses the site for its suitability. You know that your wedding will be a certain size and formality. You'll need to choose the best site not only to fit your vision as far as appearance goes, but to fulfill the other more specific needs of an event. Here, then, are the questions to ask when investigating any reception site:

- Is it available on your wedding date?
- Will there be any other weddings going on there at the same time?
- Is another wedding closely booked before or after yours?
- Is there a soundproof wall between parties?
- Is it truly soundproof?
- Will the room be set up the night before or hours before?
- Is the room large enough to fit your guests comfortably?
- Is the dance floor big enough?
- Does the site provide enough tables, chairs, linens, and other rented items?
- How is the lighting?
- How are the acoustics?
- How is the view through any large windows?
- Are there fire exits?

- Is it handicapped accessible?
- Are the bathrooms clean, attractive, and in good working order?
- Is there a separate suite for the bride, groom, and bridal party for the cocktail hour?
- Is there a separate room for the cocktail hour?
- Is there adequate parking in the parking lot?
- Is there a nearby parking lot?
- Is there valet service?
- Is there coat-check service?
- Do they have a liquor license?
- Have they been inspected for health codes?
- Are they a non-smoking building?
- Is there a smoking area, perhaps by the bar?
- Do they have insurance?
- Have they been reviewed by any major or local press?

Of course, you will have to view each site in person to get a good feel for the room and the location. It is your wedding vision, so you will have to see how the site feels to you. Your top priority may be that the room is attractive, and you know that it will be decorated more thoroughly when it's designed for your wedding, but you do need to make sure the little details such as working toilets are in place.

One great piece of advice I can lend you is to view the room when it is set up for another wedding. Ask the location manager if you can pop in a half hour before another wedding celebration is set to begin. He should have no problem with that, if you promise not to pick out of the shrimp cocktail bowl. Take a good look around, make sure the tables are set well, the staff is busily perfecting the arrangements, and the food displays meet your expectations.

Only then, with that first-hand experience, can you book your reception site. Never book from looking at pictures or asking questions over the phone, never book a place that you know to have been nice five years ago, and never book purely on a friend's recommendation. This is one of the most important jobs of the wedding, so put your all into it.

Chapter 5

Choosing the Bridal Party

For your first wedding, you may have had a large number of bridal attendants. According to *Bridal Guide*, the average number of bridesmaids for a first wedding is six. Six women in pale peach gowns, standing in places of honor for you as you walked down the aisle. They may have been your sisters, your group of best friends since college, or your groom's sisters and brothers on the men's side.

A great deal of first weddings see enormous bridal parties—some as large as 12 bridesmaids and 12 ushers. After all, the bride and groom do not want to leave anyone out. They each have siblings and siblings-in-law, as well as entire groups of best friends. No one can be left out of their bridal party, as that is the stuff that ruins friendships. One bride tearfully remembered her grandmother calling her up and yelling at her for not having all of her cousins in the bridal party. This bride already had 10 bridesmaids and ushers, and including the eight cousins would have given her wedding a parade-like quality.

Indeed, the first time around presents many headaches about whom to include in the honored lineup, who will be offended if left out, and where to draw the line. Some couples even argue over each other's choices of honor attendants. One bride recalls, "I didn't want him to include his two frat buddies who I hated. I knew they were going to be unruly, if not drunk, at the wedding, and I didn't want them ruining my day. But it was his decision."

With a sigh, this bride symbolizes the diplomatic headaches faced by most couples during a first wedding when it comes to forming the bridal party. The choices may not be their own. Parents certainly have something to say about including relatives and friends: "My father actually told me that bridal parties are for family only," says one groom, more amused than frustrated. "The memories and the pictures last forever, he said, and the friendships I have now may not last forever."

Such is the struggle of the first-time marrying couple. Whom to include? How many to include? What's the rule about having so many ushers per so many guests? What if there is an unequal number of ushers to bridesmaids? Can I have a maid and a matron of honor? I've heard it all, and I'll remind you again: The beauty of being a second-time bride is that you can choose whomever you want. It is almost a given considering the circumstances that you will not have an enormous bridal party, and you are not in that young stage right out of college where everyone is in everyone else's lineups. Now, you're more mature, you're not as swayed by others' decisions, and you rightly put your own wants and needs above what others will think, say, and do. So the choices are yours.

The trends in second-time bridal parties

Diane Forden of *Bridal Guide* says that most second-time brides are opting away from the big, all-inclusive bridal parties and choosing instead a maid of honor and one or two close friends as attendants. If the bride or groom have children, the children are included as attendants, and they may be the only ones in the party. That makes for a lovely, unified gathering, symbolic in its exclusivity.

Other brides are choosing to have a maid or matron of honor—which is vital, as honor attendants must be there to act as witnesses in the signing of the marriage certificate—but they are surrounding themselves with a small group of flower girls instead of bridesmaids. This is a wonderful choice, provided your flower girls are ages 6 to 10 and well-behaved. The look of a bride surrounded by ringlet-haired flower girls in pretty, sashed dresses is a memorable one, and even advertisers on Madison Avenue go for this vision in their memorable television campaigns. Most brides say their photos with the children look angelic, and they love to be surrounded by the innocence and joy of a youthful group of little girls.

This is not to say that you cannot have a large bridal party. Perhaps your first wedding was a small affair, and you had only one or two maids. This time, you're getting the full-on wedding with all of the trimmings, and you want the big bridal party. As mentioned earlier, you have the complete freedom to make that choice.

The politics of the invitation

It's always a special moment when the bride and groom ask their closest friends and relatives to stand up for them at the wedding. But in a second wedding, there may be some touchy politics involved. Do you ask the same bridesmaids to stand up for you again? What if you've drifted somewhat from one of them over the years and now feel strange about asking her to join in again? Do you ask his sisters to join the list when you're not particularly close, or if there is some tension between you? Do you leave them out, doing what's best for your internal wishes, and then face the wrath of their exclusion?

Many brides report that this second-time situation means a great deal of sticky interpersonal questions. On the one hand, they want what they want, but on the other hand, they don't want to start family feuds or ruin old friendships. So how does the choosing and asking get done in a way that's pleasing and acceptable to everyone?

The first step is to discuss your plans with your fiancé. If you're sure you want a small bridal party, including just your sisters this time, tell him your plans and ask for him to support you when his mother presses for other inclusions. Explain that you do not want to have a circus procession this time around, that it's important to you to just have a select group of your closest relatives.

Next, ask the women on your list if they would like to participate. Most likely they will, but you'll have to be prepared for ambivalence or even a rejection. Remember, being in a bridal party costs money and time—both precious commodities in every busy woman's life. You, and your groom when he asks his men, are asking for their inclusion. You're expressing your wishes. But be prepared to hear no.

How attendants feel about being asked

It may be surprising, but you might find that some of your friends may actually be relieved that they are not being asked to serve in your new bridal party. Many of the women I spoke to said the following:

> "I love my friend Sarah with all my heart, and I'm happy she's getting married. I know she sweated not asking me to be a bridesmaid this time around, and she was so nervous when she was kind of avoiding the issue with me. But I just smiled and said that I was happy not to be

in the party this time. I would be at her wedding and share the day with her, but I just didn't have the money to be a bridesmaid again. I'd been in several bridal parties that year, and all those ugly dresses cleaned out my account. We talked about it, she felt much better, and we're still the best of friends."

—Marianne

"I hate being a bridesmaid, so I was relieved when I found out I didn't "make" the list. First of all, I don't have the money to throw showers, buy dresses I'll never wear again, go in on expensive gifts, and so on. I don't mind not being in the honored lineup, because I can just enjoy the day, not have to pose for pictures and have other duties, and I can wear a more flattering dress. I know it sounds selfish, but I am there to support Marie and Todd 100 percent, to share their day and be happy for them. I don't need to have my name listed in the program again."

—Tia

"I didn't expect to get asked in the first place. We're not college room-mates anymore, we have our own lives, we talk once a month, and although we're still the best of friends, it didn't even enter my mind that I should be in her bridal party. So it wasn't a big deal."

—Anita

The responses of many of these brides' friends are a good representa-tion of the attitudes you may face when letting your bridal party choices be known. Most people will not be surprised, most will not challenge you, and most will be relieved to not have to "work" on your wedding day. So, the politics may not be as challenging as you think.

You know in your heart whom you want to have in your bridal party. It may simply be your children, the person who introduced you and your fiancé to one another, and your best friend. It may be the one sister you're closest to. Whatever your choice, you can avoid the politics game by mak-ing your selections with confidence, not giving anyone else veto power over those selections, and being happy about having the bridal party you want. You may get feedback from detractors, but think about it: You're not that first-time bride who is eager to please everyone else. This is your wedding, and choosing your honor attendants is a very important task. It is up to you and no one else.

When your maid of honor is a man

Having an honor attendant of the opposite gender is actually quite common now. More and more brides and grooms are choosing their closest friends to be their Best Person, and their closest friends may be someone of the opposite sex.

If your closest pal is a man, you may choose to have him stand on your side as your attendant. He, of course, will wear the standard men's attire for the wedding. On the groom's side, he may choose his best female friend as his attendant. It is a common thing now, and few people are surprised by the choice. So do not be swayed by public opinion or speculation, discuss this option with your fiancé, and bestow the honor where you see fit.

Bridal party choice criteria

During the planning of your first wedding, when making out your bridal party list, you probably just grouped together your sisters, your friends, his sisters, and so on. You may have chosen people because you were in their bridal parties. Your fiancé may have wanted those dreaded frat buddies in his lineup. Overall, the first bridal party is chosen more on a level of status and as a *reflection of who the couple is at the time*. Very often, the first-time couple is young, more affected by their outward definitions in relations to others, controlled by their parents' wishes, and bound by the rules of group inclusion within their social cliques.

Now that you've matured and your life has changed, you may not be so bound to those rules. The selection of your bridal party may go by different criteria, such as who is closest to you now, who helped you through your divorce, and who in your family is closest to you. You're looking at attendants for what they can bring to your attendant circle rather than making the choice according to whom you can't leave out.

Most couples I spoke to said they also looked at their bridal parties in terms of their roles for the big day. Sure, it's easy to pick a group of siblings to wear the outfits and look pretty in the pictures, but what about the responsibilities of the day? The seating of guests? Making introductions? Running out at the last minute to buy another pair of stockings? Who has the best qualities of a good attendant?

You're not interviewing for these spots, but you might want to follow the lead of other couples who made their bridal party choices according to these criteria:

- Level of responsibility. Will this person return size cards on time? Show up for fittings?
- Financial situation. Are they in deep debt with college loans, alimony, a job loss? Can they afford the burden of buying dresses and accessories, renting tuxes, throwing parties, giving gifts?
- Availability. Can your best friend fly in from Singapore for the wedding?
- Social graces. Will your attendants mingle, or will they sit in the corner with their brooding biker boyfriend that you don't like? Are the groom's frat buddies likely to show up drunk at the rehearsal and act like idiots, not taking the whole thing seriously? Choose someone whose demeanor matches the formality of the event.
- Acceptance of your marriage. If your sister isn't happy about your marrying your fiancé, she may show her displeasure by being difficult or unexpressive during the day. If she has taken the joy out of your plans, do not honor her with a position in your bridal party.

Bridal party responsibilities

Even if everyone in your wedding party has been a bridesmaid or an usher before, and they know the drill about what they're supposed to do when, the conditions change if you are not having the kind of traditional wedding that they're used to being involved with. Your wedding may be unique, and you may choose to have your bridal party play other roles in addition to the ones always printed in books and magazines.

Here, then, is a list of those traditional responsibilities, with space for you to fill in the extra responsibilities you'd like to assign to your attendants. Just use this list as a starting point to get you thinking about where you might need them to help, or where you might want to spotlight their talents and personalities. Remember, though, that there's a difference between setting a responsibility and asking for a favor. So do not *assign* the task of making party favors, but rather ask for help with the job. Some additional responsibilities you might list are picking up relatives from the airport, picking up the flower order on the wedding morning, helping to assemble the tent and arrange the rented chairs and tables, bringing the gifts home after the reception, and so on.

Maid/matron of honor

- Help bride choose wedding gown.
- Help organize fittings schedules for the bridesmaids.
- Arrange bridesmaids' gown payment schedules.
- Help bridesmaids order shoes and accessories.
- Plan shower or brunch for the bride.
- Attend bridal brunch on morning of wedding.
- Arrive early on morning of wedding to help bride dress.
- Participate in pre-wedding photo shoot.
- Walk in processional for wedding ceremony.
- Hold bride's bouquet and groom's ring during the ceremony.
- Witness the signing of the marriage certificate.
- Stand in the receiving line.
- Participate in post-wedding photo shoot.
- Act as social hostess during reception.
- Be available to run last-minute errands or make emergency confirmation phone calls.
- Pay for wardrobe and accessories.
- Pay for own travel and lodging.
- Other:
- Other:
- Other:

Bridesmaids

- Attend shopping trip for bridesmaids' gowns.
- Make payments and provide ordering information for bridesmaids' gowns.
- Schedule and attend fittings.
- Order and purchase shoes and accessories.
- Assist maid/matron of honor in planning the shower.
- Attend the shower.
- Arrive at bride's home for bridal brunch on wedding morning.
- Get dressed at bride's home on wedding morning.
- Participate in pre-wedding photo shoot.
- Participate in the processional.

- Participate in the wedding ceremony as directed.
- Participate in the recessional.
- Stand in the receiving line.
- Participate in post-wedding photo shoot.
- Act as social hostesses during the reception.
- Be available for last-minute errands, phone calls, or requests.
- Pay for wedding wardrobe and accessories.
- Pay for own travel and lodging.
- Other:
- Other:
- Other:

Best man:

- Help groom select and order tuxedoes.
- Organize ushers' ordering, payment, fittings, and pickup of tuxedoes, shoes, and accessories.
- Plan bachelor party (optional).
- Spend morning with the groom, keeping him calm and occupied.
- Help groom get his tie and accessories right.
- Drive groom to ceremony site.
- Bring license and rings to ceremony.
- Participate in the ceremony.
- Participate in the recessional.
- Stand in the receiving line (optional).
- Participate in post-wedding photo shoot.
- Act as social host at reception.
- Propose toast to bride and groom.
- Be available for last-minute errands, phone calls, or troubleshooting.
- Drive couple to honeymoon suite (optional).
- Arrange to have tuxedoes returned to rental shop.
- Pay for own wardrobe.
- Pay for own travel and lodging.
- Other:
- Other:
- Other:

Ushers and groomsmen:

- ❧ Attend tuxedo fittings.
- ❧ Pay for tuxedo rental.
- ❧ Pick up tuxedoes, shoes, and accessories on chosen day.
- ❧ Help plan bachelor party (optional).
- ❧ Arrive at ceremony site one hour early to seat guests according to directions.
- ❧ Help keep groom calm.
- ❧ Escort groom's mother to her seat.
- ❧ Escort bride's mother to her seat.
- ❧ Roll out white carpet (optional).
- ❧ Take places for processional.
- ❧ Participate in wedding ceremony.
- ❧ Participate in recessional.
- ❧ Stand in receiving line (optional).
- ❧ Pose for post-wedding photos.
- ❧ Act as social hosts at reception.
- ❧ Pay for own wardrobe, shoes, and accessories.
- ❧ Pay for own travel and lodging.
- ❧ Other:
- ❧ Other:
- ❧ Other:

Chapter 6

Legal and Religious Requirements

L ike it or not, a marriage is a legal partnership that has to be recognized by the state, at the very least. If you are religious people, you may also need your union to be recognized as valid by your church or synagogue. Because you are marrying for the second time (or more), you may face some legal and religious challenges that first-timers do not have to face. In addition, you will have to face the standard licensing and testing procedures that your state has set up for all marriages.

In this section, you'll learn about the many facets of religious and legal requirements, so that you can make sure your marriage is a legitimate one. It may take some legwork to gather up the paperwork, and you may need to spend some extra time getting the appropriate information and, perhaps, counseling. But in the end, it will all be worth it when you do not have to face any red tape or surprise revelations about your marriage not being a "real" one in the eyes of church or state.

Religious requirements

All religious institutions have rules about performing marriage rites for people who have been married before. They will need to see proof of divorce and/or proof of annulment, so that they know you can be married in their institution.

Proof of annulment

If you have gotten an annulment, you'll need to provide the certificate you've received from your church. If you did *not* get an annulment at the time of your divorce, you may need to follow through with that action now. Many churches will not marry people whose previous marriages have not been annulled; divorce may not be enough.

In this case, you will need to meet with your pastor and explain your need for an annulment. In most cases, you will be presented with forms to fill out, in which you'll provide all the basic information about yourself, your ex, and the terms of your breakup. In some religious houses, you will also have to provide a detailed essay or answer essay questions regarding the state of your marriage and the conditions of your divorce. Some people say that this process is intrusive, that answering personal questions such as these did rub them the wrong way. Why does the church need to know about your upbringing, your childhood, and how you met your ex? Why does a description of your courtship count? As unpleasant as this step may be, and as uncomfortable as you may feel about giving out personal information, most churches unfortunately require this step.

Once you complete your application for an annulment, you may need to speak with the priest or chancellor, submit a fee, and then wait for the archdiocese to process your request. In some cases, this takes weeks. In others, it may take months.

If you are devoted to marrying in the church again, you will have to take this step. Do not worry about needing your ex's involvement and co-operation. In most cases, you can acquire an annulment without his help.

Proof of divorce

In most cases, you'll have to present a certified copy of your divorce settlement and decree. Because you may only have your own copy, you may need to contact your county courthouse for certified copies of this record. It may take a small fee and a short waiting period for delivery, but it's best to have the certified copy with the raised seal and notary public's signature before you embark on your plans. In most cases, a photocopy of your own divorce decree is not sufficient for the necessary permissions for this wedding. Most churches will not accept you as a candidate for marriage rites without this proof, and many priests want to see what the terms of your divorce were. Some may have reservations about marrying you again, and in so doing granting you the church's blessing, if you were proven to be the adulterer in your previous relationship. It may not sound fair, but many priests and rabbis take your personal history and mistakes into consideration here.

Counseling

One of the conditions of being married in a house of worship that is faced by all couples choosing this type of venue is pre-marital counseling with the officiant. It may be a standard, required course such as pre-Cana classes (in which couples meet for several sessions to discuss their inner feelings about faith, communication, child-rearing ideals, and so on), or it may be a simple matter of two or three meetings with the priest. It all depends upon your particular house of worship. So discuss the counseling requirements with your pastor, priest, or rabbi before booking your marriage at that site.

Interfaith marriages

If you and your fiancé are of different religious backgrounds and you want to incorporate elements of both faiths into your wedding (as so many couples do now), you will have to do some extra research about the requirements of such a combination. In most cases, a Catholic priest will agree to perform rites in conjunction with a rabbi if the couple so requests and complies with all planning and counseling. This is very common, and most officiants are well versed in this kind of request. Be sure to get all of the required information, plan well, interview well, and ask about special fees for the officiants to perform your ceremony at a non-religious site.

You will see in some magazines or newspapers and on some Web sites advertisements for officiants who are licensed in, or specialize in, interfaith weddings. Their credentials lists are large, their affiliations are impressive, and they seem to answer all of your prayers as far as fitting the requirements for your individual religious needs. Just be careful. Interview well. Get proof of their affiliation. Double-check their credits. Ask for referrals. Meet with them and interview them. Ask if you can look in on another ceremony they are scheduled to perform. Treat these officiants as any other wedding professionals whom you do not have previous experience with; subject them to the scrutiny that your wedding deserves for its own legitimacy and quality.

Special ordinations

Did you know that in some states, regular ordinary citizens can become ordained for the day and are thus able to perform legal wedding ceremonies? This is the case right now in California, and one couple who chose to have their best friend ordained for them said it was a wonderful, personal touch for their union. The friend did an outstanding job, and the wedding was more meaningful because the officiant knew the couple and could speak of them with knowledge and familiarity. Check with your town hall about the rules of special ordinations.

Legal requirements

Of course you know a marriage has to be legal, but in your case the issues go far beyond the creation of a marriage license. You will need to be sure you have proof of your divorce or proof of the death of your previous spouse in order for the state to recognize your marriage in this case. Whether or not your wedding will be held in a religious setting, a non-religious setting, or at a Justice of the Peace, you'll need to apply officially and provide proof of your marrying status.

If your divorce is still pending, you will need to hasten the process along, or at least plan this second wedding for after your divorce is finalized. Some brides have had to postpone their weddings due to a delay in getting that final paperwork from the legal actions of the divorce. Bigamy rules apply if you do not.

Again, obtain certified copies of your divorce papers or your spouse's death certificate from the county courthouse. Have several copies in hand, because filing may require copies submitted to several levels of courts or license bureaus, such as your town hall.

In some cases, you may need copies of your birth certificate as well. Couples who plan to marry on cruises or at international locations do have a larger burden of identification to prove, and birth certificates are a common requirement for many destinations. If you do not have a copy of your birth certificate, you will need to contact the records department of the hospital where you were born. Provide all of your personal information, submit the application form and fee, and you should receive certified copies of your birth certificate in a matter of weeks. Again, it depends upon the rules and speed of service in your area.

Special testing

You are probably aware from your first marriage that sometimes certain blood tests need to be taken before the marriage license can be issued. All states have different testing requirements, and *your state's requirements may have changed since you were last married.* So do not go by old information that you may still have on hand from years ago. Call your town hall for testing requirements or for a referral to your state's marriage licensing bureau, and ask about the tests that are required.

In many states, HIV testing is a standard, but some states also require testing for syphilis, hepatitis, and other conditions. What is most important to note and schedule is the time periods and location requirements for these tests. Most states have a window of time for your testing to be valid. In other words, you must have your blood work done by a licensed facility a certain amount of time before the wedding itself. Results may only be valid for a month or two.

Another question to ask concerns the location of your wedding. If you will be married in your old home state of Florida, but you live in New York City, will your blood taken in New York City be considered valid by the Florida marriage-licensing bureau? What about international rules? Will your foreign destination accept your United States testing results? Ask these questions of the licensing bureau in the location where you will be married, and allow plenty of time to schedule testing and receive results. This takes some intricate planning, but it is a must.

Prenuptial agreements

I know, the words send shivers down your spine. No one really likes to start off her marriage plans with such an unromantic issue such as this. Many people find pre-nups to be a big dark cloud over what is supposed to be a blissful time of trust, optimism, and celebration. It is a veritable statement of "What if this doesn't work out?" and no one likes to have to face that possibility.

This is a time, however, where men and women have their own assets. Sometimes they may be significant ones, and everyone likes to protect his or her own interests. Especially in the case of second or third marriages, where there are children born of each person's previous relationship, the future allocation of money and goods becomes a very large issue. For some people, the drawing up of a valid pre-nuptial agreement is a sigh of relief, signifying that "What's mine is mine, what's yours is yours, and what's ours is ours." It does give a measure of equality to the marriage, and no one has any unspoken fears about what might happen someday. Legal paperwork has taken care of it in black and white.

Others resent the proposition of a pre-nup, taking it personally as an accusation of greed. Such a person might feel, "How could you think I would be a gold-digger?" This causes many fights, many simmering issues, and even the first plantings of doubt about the other person's character and trust level.

What is important to note is that establishing a prenuptial agreement is entirely up to the two of you, and it does take one of the most serious discussions of your lives to make the decision. You will both have to think about what the pre-nup means to you personally and in the form of realistic protection of your *own* belongings. As I mentioned earlier, these are not times when the man has it all and the woman is out to land a good financial provider. We live in an age where women can provide for themselves, do not need men to take care of them, and have savings, investments, trust funds, assets, and 401(k)s of their own to look after. They may have children who would be happy to hear that the new husband is not first in line to inherit the goods. It sounds harsh, but when it comes to money, family relationships can get skewed. So take the time now to discuss the need for a pre-nup, the terms, the execution of it, and its ultimate fairness to both of you.

As in all matters of law, the rules may vary from state to state. Georgia, for instance, does not issue prenuptial agreements. Your state is likely to have its standard application processes, and the highest quality attorneys should be consulted for the creation of your paperwork. Do *not* rely on computer-generated, do-it-yourself pre-nups, as they may not be enforceable in the future.

Family law and divorce attorney Brett Levine, of Levine and Levine Attorneys in Florham Park, New Jersey offers the following general advice for the creation of a valid and fair prenuptial agreement.

- Find a qualified legal representative with membership in your state's bar association for the creation of a complete, valid document.
- Know what your personal wishes are for the prenuptial agreement. Be sure that the two of you have discussed all the terms of your agreement and that both of you are comfortable with what you are agreeing to.

- Take your time planning this step, as it should not be rushed.
- Allow time for the document to be processed and run through the legal system before the wedding. Several months' advance time should suffice.
- Judges do not like prenuptial agreements that stipulate that one partner automatically gets custody of the children or that one partner will not have to pay support in the event of a divorce. Any prenup that gives one person all rights to everything can be termed invalid in court by the Uniform Premarital Agreement Act, which is enforceable in most states.
- Do not sign, or be pressured to sign, a pre-nuptial agreement the day before the wedding. That too can be overturned in court as evidence of a pressured decision.
- Judges generally view pre-nups as tools of manipulation. They are far more likely to honor your requests made through more standard legal documents such as wills, deeds, and guardianships.

This last rule will serve you best. You may choose to handle your future affairs through wills and deeds, as that legal process may be more comfortable to you. A prenuptial agreement definitely introduces a big "what if?" into your marriage, and it can have a large effect on your future. I have spoken to many couples, both married and divorced, and found their stories vary to great degrees. Some wish they had established fair prenuptial agreements before their weddings to protect them from shark attacks on their assets after a bitter divorce. Some wish they hadn't signed a manipulative document out of starry-eyed love and loyalty to a partner. The individual stories all depend greatly on the individuals involved in them, how long they were engaged, the character of the couple, what kind of assets each had, and if there was a great difference in income level between the two. This is why I urge you to consider your own financial situation, think about what's best for you and for your children, discuss the issue with your partner, and get a fair legal document drawn up if you do decide to go this route. And do remember Levine's words (which are especially handy in a friendly and calm negotiation of this topic with your fiancé): All issues are best handled through wills, deeds, and guardianships.

It is a great thing to be able to love and trust your partner, but it is a greater thing to love and trust yourself enough to keep control over what's yours.

Name change options

Speaking of what's yours, you may be among those second-time brides who take on their fiancé's last name. Or you may join the growing number of people who both hyphenate their names together. In some cases, marrying parents ask their children if the kids want to take on the last name of their new stepparent, and that does happen from time to time. Whatever the condition, as varied as conditions can be these days, you may enter into the world of name changes.

At the time of your marriage, your wedding license is valid for the submission of name change forms. For your children, some paperwork may have to be filed at the courthouse, and you may have to appear before a judge for the changes to take place. Again, it all depends upon the rules of your state.

In any case, you'll need to make sure you change your name with the following agencies, companies, and services:

- Bank accounts.
- Credit card accounts.
- Investment accounts.
- Wills, trusts, deeds, and guardianships.
- Driver's license.
- Car registration and AAA-type plans.
- Social security account.
- Insurance accounts.
- Work benefits and employee records.
- Doctors' and dentists' offices.
- Passport.
- Telephone company.
- Cable company.
- Voter registration.
- Library card.
- Magazine subscriptions.
- Professional and social organizations.
- Computer accounts.
- Relatives.
- Friends.

As far as other legal requirements, check with your local marriage licensing bureau to find out the latest requirements of your state so that you are up to date, organized, and creating a wonderful, valid marriage.

Chapter 7

Planning the Ceremony

The legalities and religious requirements of your wedding are a necessary issue to deal with, but the heart of the planning is in creating a wedding ceremony that is an expression of your union. You marriage may be made valid with the signing of a license, and it may be recognized by your religion with the taking of vows, but the elements of the entire ceremony itself are what make the marriage legitimate and meaningful to *you*.

During the planning of your first wedding, the ceremony steps may have been dictated to you by the boundaries of your church, synagogue, officiant, or even your parents. You may have had a little bit of room for personalization with the music selections you made, the readings you chose, and the words you cut out of the standard vows. But this time, the ceremony is more under your direction, more under your control. The entire realm of the ceremony is up to you to create according to your adherence to traditional practices or your desire to break out of the mold and plan something completely original.

In this section, you'll consider each of the main parts of the ceremony, and you'll plan for the statements, symbolism, and expressions you wish to incorporate. All of the details are up to you (with some exceptions regarding the absolute rules imposed by some religious and site restrictions). You have far more freedom this time than last to plan a ceremony that speaks of your personalities, your commitment, and the nature of your relationship and hopes for the future.

Religious or non-religious

As mentioned earlier, you may choose to hold your wedding ceremony in a traditional religious setting, going by the bounds of the traditional service, or you may opt for a more secular wedding, without the rites and prayers. After all, you may not be a very religious person, and it would be more of a statement of your own beliefs to apply the individual faith you've come to rely on, whether it be a more universal faith rather than an established one or a complete absence of religion in the ceremony.

In today's society, there is a definite establishment of non-religious people, and they have a right to wedding ceremonies that do not force words or beliefs into their mouths. As an older and more self-assured person, you may choose this option. You may decide to plan with your officiant a completely secular ceremony. This will require an honest discussion with him so that he can assess which beliefs you hold and which you do not hold. Officiants are more savvy these days. They know that not everyone is part of an established religion, and they do their best to help create a wedding ceremony that is a true reflection of the couple's beliefs.

Choosing an officiant

This may be a simple step if you have decided to go the traditional religious route in loyalty to your established faith and membership in a church or synagogue. In this case, it may not be a case of choosing the right officiant, but rather finding a date that your favorite pastor is available. You may have a wonderful, longtime relationship with your religious leader, and you would consider no other officiant for your wedding ceremony.

For those who don't have a favorite member of the clergy, or those whose individual wedding plans restrict their first choice from participating in some way, there begins an interview and selection process. You'll have to investigate, ask questions, and make wise choices to find a quality officiant for the performance of your wedding rites, and your task will depend on what you are looking for. Do you want a religious leader in a non-religious setting? Do you want two religious leaders to handle the double realms of an interfaith wedding? Do you want a simple appearance before a judge to get the ceremony out of the way with little fuss? Whatever your personal requirements, all officiants must be subjected to the same scrutiny that you'll give other wedding professionals. It is necessary that you select the right officiant for you, one who allows you the freedom to create the ceremony you want.

Non-religious officiants

If you and your partner do not wish to go the religious route with your wedding, but would instead prefer a secular officiant, you have many options open to you. You may choose to have your ceremony performed by a Justice of the Peace, a judge, or a mayor, all of whom are licensed to perform marriage ceremonies.

All it takes to find a suitable officiant is a quick call to your local county courthouse to inquire about your state's rules and requirements. In most cases, a judge of the municipal, state, or supreme level will be available to perform a "quickie" ceremony for a small price. These judges perform marriages on a regular basis as part of their dockets, and although you may not get the option of a lot of personalization in your ceremony, you will be married legally with a minimum of fuss in a short time. Usually, these ceremonies are held within judges' chambers or in a courthouse, and you may have anyone you like present to observe. Most judges will meet with you privately shortly before the ceremony to discuss your wishes for wording, but the rites are pretty much standard.

Many brides and grooms do not like the courthouse setting, reminiscent as it may be of their divorces or other legal wranglings. Instead, they may choose to have a non-religious officiant perform their ceremony at a location other than the courthouse. Many judges and mayors are willing to come to your location to act as officiant, but it takes a bit of effort and planning to work your event into their schedules. So be flexible and take time to search well for the right officiant for you.

As for finding a mayor, simply call your local town hall and ask the mayor's assistant for a printed list of the requirements, waiting periods, fees, and availablity. Mayors, in my opinion, do fine jobs of performing marriage ceremonies. As politicians, they are great speakers, and they usually look forward to performing weddings as a fun part of their jobs. Some put their all into it, and most brides say that their delivery is far preferable to that of a judge who is going by rote.

A third option is a licensed marriage officiant listed in your phone book's yellow pages. Some brides and grooms do brave this list from time to time, although I have heard stories of hired officiants who were not actually licensed. You may find the perfect New Age officiant here, but check references fully and be sure the person is licensed and professional enough to incorporate your wishes into the ceremony.

Couples who marry on ships or yachts may have their ceremonies performed and validated by the ship's captain. Be sure, though, to follow through on research with your county courthouse to verify the potential legality of your marriage in your state of record.

Interviewing officiants

Begin your search by addressing the main issues of availability:

- Are you available on our wedding date?
- Are you available at the time of our wedding?
- How many other weddings are you doing that day?
- Do you have the amount of time we require?

Next, ask about the particulars of what you want, and whether the officiant can handle your requests:

- Do you perform ceremonies at outside locations (such as our home, the beach, etc.)?
- Do you perform non-religious ceremonies?
- Do you perform interfaith ceremonies?
- Will you perform the ceremony with another religious leader?
- Do you offer bilingual services?
- Will you allow us to choose our own ceremony elements?
- Will you allow us to write our own vows?
- Will you allow our children to participate in the ceremony?

Next come the more personal issues:

- Is the officiant licensed to perform ceremonies?
- Does the officiant have adequate experience in performing ceremonies such as yours?
- Does the officiant speak well and present himself well?
- Does the officiant allow you to express what you want of your ceremony?
- Does the officiant make you feel at ease?
- Does the officiant grill you about your personal relationship—or lack thereof—to the church? Many brides report that some officiants act reluctant to handle their wedding if the couple is not affiliated to a great degree with the officiant's house of worship.

Now, the business end:

- ❧ What are your fees?
- ❧ Do we have to make a donation to your church?
- ❧ What documentation do you require of us?
- ❧ Do we have to attend counseling with you?
- ❧ How many meetings must we have with you?

In the end, if you have chosen the right officiant, the grounds are set for you to make all of the choices you wish for your ceremony. The right officiant will not limit your choices, impose his own personal rules on your service, or make you feel as if you're burdening him with the details of planning your wedding. Susan, a recent bride, shares her story:

"The new priest at my church was so rude when we called to ask him about my fiancé's annulment papers. He stalled us, he gave us the runaround, and he actually told me that I was not a recognized member of his church! My money had been good there for years, I taught Sunday school there, my nieces were baptized there, and I went to the Catholic school affiliated with that church when I was younger. I knew it was simply a case of having to deal with a bad priest—and there are bad eggs in every profession—so we asked for another priest and were happily married in my church. Do not let the wrong officiant bully you, or you won't have the wedding you want."

Personalizing the ceremony

Now that you have the officiant who will guide the ceremony, it's time to create the ceremony itself. The most important parts are the vows, but the rest of the elements create the meaning of the ritual and will remain in your memory as the expression of your partnership. How lucky you are to have the freedom now to design and detail the pieces of your ceremony so that it flows as you like it, so that all the words ring true, so that the promises you make are truly yours. How amazing that you will bring into the picture the people who are most meaningful to you, and that your children will be an important part of the day. So let's get started with the planning.

Who will participate

We'll begin with the issue of having your children be a vital and highly involved part of your wedding. Wedding experts speak with emotion about

the involvement of the children of the partners, and family therapists em-
phasize how meaningful it is to bring the kids into the picture as a support
to the establishment of a new family unit. This is not just the joining of you
and your husband-to-be; it's the joining of both your families into one new
one, the creation of a new bond. A wedding is a ritual in itself, but when
children are a part of the wedding, the ritual takes on a whole new dimension. Kids need this official statement to spell out the definition of their
family. They also need to hear you say openly that they will all be treated
with love and respect and as equals. They'll need to hear that the family
structure that will be created will be a solid one for them, and that they are
not going to be lost in the shuffle. Involving children of any age to a great
degree in the wedding is the best beginning to your new life together, for
you, for them, and for your foundation as a cohesive family.

Depending upon your children's ages and maturity levels—and their
feelings about the union—consider asking them to participate in any of the
following roles:

- Escorting you down the aisle.
- Walk down the aisle scattering rose petals or confetti.
- Giving you away.
- Being the ring bearer.
- Reading poetry or psalms.
- Writing and delivering a reading at the ceremony.
- Performing music.
- Presenting the "gifts" as part of a religious ceremony.
- Helping to light the unity candle.
- Taking family vows.

Your children should be made a large part of the ceremony as individuals. It's an important statement to make for them. They may appreciate your honoring them for their acceptance of the union, for treating them
as important members of the wedding, and for giving them the chance to
share in the attention and symbolism of the day.

If you do not have children, you may choose to have other important
people in your life do the readings, perform music, give a short speech, or
even walk you down the aisle. One bride shared with me the story of how a
special family friend created a professionally edited videotape of her and
her fiancé over the years of their courtship. He had used childhood photos
of them, video footage of their engagement, and other enjoyable images

set to a musical soundtrack as a special gift and presentation at the beginning of the wedding. This personal touch was enjoyed by all, and the ceremony itself took on new meaning for those guests who may not have known one member of the couple very well before that day.

The readings

Most wedding ceremonies include readings as part of the service. Whether or not they are religious in nature is up to you. You may choose to include your favorite psalms or the ever-popular Corinthians 13: "…and the greatest of these is love." Second-time brides do, however, like to stay away from the readings they had at their first ceremonies, and because Corinthians is such a standard choice, other readings may be selected to take its place.

You may choose poetry by Elizabeth Barrett Browning ("How do I love thee? Let me count the ways"), or use original poetry you've written yourself. You may select readings from a work of spiritual messages that speak to who you are now, such as elements from Oriah Mountain Dreamer's renowned book *The Invitation* or Marianne Williamson's *Illuminata*. You can find any brand of poetry, essays, lengthy quotes, or even play stanzas from Shakespeare online or in your library. You can find a wide selection of popular and wedding readings in a book titled *Wedding Readings* by Eleanor Munro. However extensive the availability of classic poetry and little-known Apache wedding blessings, the most popular option at second weddings is original readings.

You may choose to read from letters you've written one another over the years. You may choose to read from your journal. Or, as some brides have chosen, ask your kids to write their own essays or poetry for reading at the wedding. Children who are into writing poetry or stories love the attention, and you get a very special, meaningful addition to your wedding.

The music

The music makes the wedding. The songs you choose for all parts of your wedding ceremony set the tone for the entire event, give your guests a feeling of peace or celebration, and speak of your personal tastes. Depending upon the style of your wedding, whether formal and classic or informal and fun, you should choose ceremony music that fits with the style of your event.

Since second-time brides are primarily older, more sophisticated, and more likely to go for a classic sound, I've collected a short list of suggested songs for each part of the standard wedding ceremony:

- **The Prelude:**
  "Water Music" by Handel.
  "Jesu, Joy of Man's Desiring," by Bach.
  "Rhapsody on a Theme by Paganini," by Rachmaninoff.

- **The Processional:**
  "Spring" (from The Four Seasons) by Vivaldi.
  "Wedding March" (from the Marriage of Figaro) by Mozart.
  "Canon in D Major" by Pachelbel.
  "Trumpet Voluntary" by Clarke.
  "Trumpet Voluntary in D" by Purcell.

- **During the Ceremony** (such as candle-lighting, preparing the gifts, before the exchange of rings):
  "Amazing Grace."
  "Ave Maria," by Bach.
  "The Prayer," by Celine Dion and Andrea Boccelli.

- **Recessional:**
  "Ode to Joy" by Beethoven.
  "The Hallelujah Chorus" (from The Messiah) by Handel.
  "Wedding March" (from A Midsummer Night's Dream) by
      Mendelssohn.

Of course, you can incorporate more modern love songs such as "You Are So Beautiful," by Joe Cocker, "It Had to Be You," by Harry Connick Jr., or any other love song that has become a part of your own romantic repertoire over the years. Some couples are having fun with their recessional music, choosing more upbeat tunes that get the guests laughing and ready to celebrate. I do recommend staying away from sexually oriented songs, as your kids will definitely not want to think about your wedding night.

Search through wedding music at the library, talk to your reception entertainment musicians for their ceremony music suggestions (they know about more than conga lines and the chicken dance), and search through musical instruction books found at your library for free sheet music to your chosen songs.

The vows

The vows are the biggest part of the ceremony. It's the promise you make to seal your partnership, which is the entire reason for the whole event you've worked so hard to plan. Again, as a second-time bride, you're not likely to go by the standard vows most first-timers use, but are more apt to create your own vows. As your wedding is your own vision, your vows should be your own words and thoughts.

You've spoken vows before. For whatever reasons, you are no longer bound by them. Now, it's time to create new vows with a new partner, a completely original set of promises and statements about the person you are now, the person you are with your partner, and the future you will have together. As you write your vows, keep several rules in mind:

1. Don't put too much pressure on yourself. Just take some time, search your feelings, and write what comes from your heart.
2. Don't make them too long. Keep it short and to the point.
3. Don't plan on memorizing them. You'll be nervous that day, and you may even forget your own name. You can arrange with the officiant for you to read your vows from a card if necessary.
4. Write about your love and commitment to one another, the promises you will keep.
5. Make your vows sound like you. If you're an emotional, expressive person, your vows will be the same. If you're more humorous, don't be afraid to put that side of your personality into your words. The best vows are those that sound like the couple wrote them, not some speechwriter.
6. Don't leave this task to the big day, thinking you'll just express what you feel at the moment. What you'll get is a stuttering, disjointed rambling that will be caught forever on videotape. Plan ahead, practice, and know your words.
7. Don't mention how happy you are now *as compared to the nightmare of your first marriage.* No reference should be made at all to your first marriage, as that should not be part of this day. Even if you feel strongly about how much happier you are this time around, keep that comparison to yourself for your fiancé's sake and for your kids' sake.

For more ideas on writing your own vows, see *The Complete Book of Wedding Vows,* by Diane Warner.

If you do have kids, it's a wonderful idea to take two sets of vows: one set to be shared between the two of you and another to be shared between the two of you and the kids. For some, the family medallion service, a popular wedding rite that joins the two families as one and bestows a special circular medallion to all members of the joined family, is very meaningful. For others, the idea of taking vows with the kids is a more personalized task. Here, then, are some rules about including children in the vows:

1. Together, as a couple, promise all of your children that you will love, respect, and support them always.
2. Address the children as a complete group, not separately as "his kids" or "her kids." A united front is needed here.
3. Allow the kids to make vows to you. Although they cannot promise that they will adhere to certain rules, and they may not know what they want to promise at this point, give them the freedom to just create their own vows according to how they feel.
4. Explain to the kids the meaning of the vows part of the ceremony, and *invite* them to participate. By all means, do not force them to make promises they don't intend to keep.
5. Don't write the vows for the kids.
6. Don't make all of the kids adhere to one set of vows, unless they write them as a group.
7. Allow them to be individuals in their expressions to you.
8. If you have a surly child who does not accept the marriage, do not invite disaster by asking him or her to grab the spotlight and make a promise of some sort. Kids can be cruel when they're hurting or afraid, and they may take their pain out on you in a very public way. So assess your children's emotional state and propensity for drama before you make the decision to give them the microphone.

Little extras

After the ceremony is over and you've made your triumphant walk back down the aisle as husband and wife, your guests will gather to make the first expression of celebration with you. Traditionally, their action has been the throwing of birdseed. As you know, rice is out because of its harmful effects on birds that eat it, and confetti is often banned from most sites due to its cleanup problem. So what's left?

Couples are now going with the following options:

- Bubbles. Very popular in the wedding industry right now, you can find these little packs of bubble containers—some decorated for wedding use—at your local craft store or online at gift and bridal sites. The craft store is less expensive.

- Bells. Little jingle bells attached to a nicely-printed thank you or acknowledgment cards can ring out the guests' congratulations as you go running by.

- Butterflies. Professional butterfly distribution companies can ship crates of live butterflies to your event for the timed release of thousands of monarchs and other types of bright butterflies. Although this is still a popular notion, some animal rights groups are balking about this practice due to some butterflies' inability to thrive in an unseasonable environment.

- Doves. The group release of white doves after the ceremony is always a dramatic and impressive statement, as doves mate for life. Just be sure to hire a reputable company with trained doves, and plan the release at the right time of day. The doves will need plenty of daylight to find their way home, and they should be released by a staff member of that company.

- Rose petals. The showering of rose petals is always a regal addition. You can get inexpensive rose petals from a wholesaler and have the flower girl distribute handfuls to the guests before you make your exit.

- A serenade. Skip the thrown items and the flying insects and birds, and just have your guests join in song as you make your way to the waiting car. Some brides report that their guests broke out in a spontaneous performance, led by the members of the bridal party.

- Church bells. If you're marrying in a church, ask the officiant if you can arrange to have the church bells played for you. Some places do this automatically, and others need a little nudge…and perhaps a fee.

Before you make any choices or purchases for your little post-wedding extras, be sure to check with the site manager or officiant about what is allowed. Some sites have restrictions about what can be thrown or released after a wedding, and you do not want your purchase to go to waste. Think about what would be best for your location, what speaks of the style of your celebration, and what fits into your image of the perfect first moments as a married couple.

Part Two

The Fun
Stuff

Chapter 8

The Wedding Gown

Forget about the old rules that say you can't wear white if you're marrying for the second or third time. The idea that white dress means the bride is a virgin is a long-standing fallacy. The origin of the white dress goes back to ancient days, when only the rich could afford white fabric as a one-time, special-occasion outfit, and the wearing of white was a symbol of affluence, status, and celebration. Besides, if everyone went by the virgin rule, not too many white dresses would be worn at weddings today at all.

The state of the wedding fashion industry is that there are no rules. Second-time brides can wear white if they so choose. First-time brides can add color to their gowns. It has all become a matter of taste, and a grand departure from the old-time rules and regulations about what color can be worn for what life stage you're in. Personal choice is the norm now, with the standard allowance made for formality, style, and location of the wedding. So try out different styles, and you can enjoy this gown selection process more than you did the first time around.

White, or not

No one will gasp if you appear in a gorgeous, white gown on the day of your wedding. The pages of bridal magazines showcase the wide range of white gowns, and even the celebrity wedding issues of magazines show second-, third-, and fourth-time brides radiant in white once again. If Cindy Crawford, the model of style, can wear white at her second wedding, so can you. However, know that you are not limited to white or ivory dresses.

Michelle Roth of Michelle Roth Studios in New York City features wedding gowns in a great palette of pastel colors. She uses French blues, pale pinks, delicate yellows, and even the gentle metallic colors of light bronzes, coppers, silvers, and golds for some extra sparkle and eye-catching accent.

Simply said, all of your color options are open. The wedding fashion houses are showing all-white designs, white with colored accents such as pink rose gatherings at the small of the back, and a wide range of blush-colored gowns that are so popular, even first-time brides are choosing them for their wedding day.

Second-time gown styles

Just as color is no longer a bound-by-the-rules issue, neither is the style of gown you may choose for your wedding. A great deal of the decision is up to you, and the wedding fashion industry is greatly aware of that. So a variety of gowns for all ages, shapes, formalities, and locations fill the shops and catalogs. "The second-time bride is so lucky now!" says Diane Forden of *Bridal Guide*. "There are so many appropriate gowns to choose from."

Whereas your first-time gown may have been something of a princess gown with the full skirt and the modest accents, the subtle neckline, and the innocent puffy sleeves, the second-time gown is more of a statement of the bride's individuality. Forden says that brides are choosing chic silk, bias-cut gowns, sheaths, A-lines, Princess gowns, and dresses with daring back plunges and more bare skin. After all, the wedding may not be in a religious setting, and the bride's gown choice may not be subject to the church's rules of no bare shoulders and the like.

Second-time brides appear now in gowns with color in the fabric and in the accents, with floral or beaded trim, back sashes, strapless cuts, a certain amount of sculpting to the drape of the back of the dress, fitted bodices, and elaborate beading and sparkle. Trains are the sweep train, if anything, as the long train is still more traditionally for the first-time bride. And didn't you hate lugging that thing around the first time anyway?

Beth Reed Ramirez of *Bride Again*, whose entire occupation is to focus on the trends of the second-time bride, reports that the encore bride can spend more on her gown. Nearly half of her readers planned to spend between $2,000 and $3,000 on their gowns, and they had some definite ideas about what they planned to wear. These readers were savvy, sophisticated, and upscale, and they wanted their gowns to reflect their position in life, their pride at who they have become, and their inner beauty. They chose their own styles, and this is the time they wanted to shine as a jewel, not as a little princess.

Ramirez says that since many second-time weddings are informal, out-door events, the brides who plan these types of celebrations are choosing a variety of suitable gowns. For the beautiful garden wedding, the bride may select a flowing ankle-length soft organza or chiffon dress with flowers or jeweled accents in her hair.

Diane Forden of *Bridal Guide* offers her suggested list of designers for those perfect second-time wedding gown picks:

- Vera Wang.
- Christosse.
- Manale.
- Diamond Collection.
- Amsale.
- Carolina Herrera.
- Priscilla of Boston.
- Elizabeth Fillmore.
- Pcter Langner.
- Michelle Roth and Co.
- Jim Hjelm.
- Lazaro.
- Lila Broude.
- Birnbaum and Bullock (she recommends them highly!).
- Ann Barge.
- Cocoe Boci (very pricy, but worth a look!).

The rules that still apply to gown choice

Although the issue of color is no longer an etiquette-defined decision, and although style is a matter of preference, the attention to formality and the suitability of your dress for the occasion still is a matter of traditional influence. Your gown must match the formality of your event, so that you are a natural part of the grand picture. Here, then, are the rules for matching your gown choice to the formality of your wedding:

- **Formal Weddings:**
  Floor-length gown.
  Long or short train.
  Detailed or simple ornamentation.
  Long veil (note: a blusher veil is not appropriate for a second-time bride) or tiara.

- **Semi-formal evening weddings:**
  Floor-length gown or cocktail-length gown.
  Shorter veil (no blusher veil) or tiara.
  Detailed or simple ornamentation.

- **Semi-formal daytime weddings:**
  Floor-length gown or cocktail-length gown.
  Shorter veil (no blusher veil) or tiara.
  More simple ornamentation.

- **Informal weddings:**
  Floor-length gown, cocktail-length gown, slipdress, or suit.
  No veil, but perhaps hair ornamentation such as jeweled hair clips.

Finding the right style for your shape

Of course, you want to look dazzling in your gown on your wedding day. You want the most beautiful dress, the perfect fit, and you want to look better than you ever have in your life. That vision can easily be created if you take the time to analyze your body style and your personal expression style. A great many brides do themselves an injustice by trying to wear a gown that is just not *them*. It may be too flouncy, too detailed, too tight, too revealing. It may make their hips look enormous and their chest look non-existent. Although you may not have access to the kinds of personal style assistants the stars do, you can act as your own fashion adviser and make the right decision for the gown that fits you best. Do not depend on the bridal salon manager or seamstress. She doesn't know you. She doesn't know your personal style. She may be able to find a dress that accents your obvious figure dimensions, but she doesn't know which parts of your silhouette you want to show off and which you want to downplay.

So begin by thinking hard about your body shape. You cannot help the way you're built—large hips, large chest, small chest, long neck—but you can take the advice of beauty experts and play up your strengths. Be realistic about your body and the shape you're in, and buy the right gown for you.

Here are some short explanations of the types of gowns you'll have to choose from:

The ball gown:	Usually a fitted bodice (plain or beaded) with a full skirt.
The sheath:	A sleek, straight, sexy gown that adheres gently to the curves of the body.
The A-line:	A fitted bodice with a smooth, gentle wider skirt and a sweep train.
The embellished dress:	Ornamentation marks the fabric design or the added beading, pearl, bandings, flowerettes, and other trimwork designed to add a bit of texture and design to the dress.

Now that you have the basic lingo for the types of gown styles that are out there, you can begin to assess your body shape as it suits the gown styles:

- Shorter or heavier brides might choose an A-line gown or a Princess style that adds height and slims.
- Dropped waists will add length to your torso.
- Full skirts will hide your heavy or jiggly lower parts, such as hips, thighs, and bottom.
- A tight, decorative bodice (with a good bra) will accent a bust you're proud of.
- A simpler, square-cut and non-décolletage neckline will minimize a large chest.
- If you have a slim, shapely, toned body, choose a sheath dress.
- Sleeveless gowns are great if your arms are in shape.

There are countless rules about the cuts and embellishments of gowns and the perfect fit on an appropriate body type. You know, you've done this before. But this time, your body may be different. You may have lost or gained weight, had children, changed your style, grown more confident with your individual body type, and may not be showing off your alluring curves. Your fashion sense, as it is right now, has to be combined with your body image for the right selection of a gown that is *you*.

Try on several different styles in the salon, be honest about how your strongest features look, and make your decision on what *you* think makes you look best.

The right fabric

Depending upon when you're shopping and the date of your wedding, you will see gowns in a great variety of fabrics. Some, quite obviously, are more appropriate for summertime weddings, and others are better for cooler weather. When considering which gown you'll wear, you'll need to take fabric into consideration.

Wedding gown designers are showcasing many different blends of silks, cottons, organzas, and satins, and you'll have to do some research to see which kinds of fabric suit your gown style, the date of your wedding, and your personal comfort level. To make this a bit easier, you should know that some fabrics are in style all year round—silk, satin, tulle, and shantung. The crisp cotton blends are also a wonderful feel, and most designers make gowns in this low-maintenance fabric for year-round styles.

So while checking out gown styles, also get a feel for the fabric you'll be wearing. You don't want anything too stiff, too heavy, too starchy, or too shiny on your wedding day. Consider price levels—some shantungs will be more expensive than simple tulle, and those crisp cotton blends are less expensive than the satin. But it all depends on the make, designer, and details of the gown itself.

The gown tests

Most brides make a mistake when they're trying on gowns. They stand on that little platform and look at themselves in the mirror, perhaps twirling around to get a back view, peering at the side silhouette. What is most important is that the gown moves with you. A beautiful gown that does not allow you comfort and freedom of movement on your wedding day is an encumbrance, and it is not the right gown for you. Alterations can be made so that the arm holes are large enough and so that the bottom of the bodice does not cut into your stomach, but certain tests should be performed on each gown:

1. See if you can sit in it. Grab a chair and do the sit test, making sure the bodice doesn't cut, the back length and details of the gown don't make it impossible to stand back up, or the layers of skirt don't get too poofy in your lap.
2. What's the view from above? Can guests see down the front of your top?

3. Can you dance in it? Yes, you may look silly dancing in the dressing room, but it's important that you can lift your arms up high enough to dance with your groom.
4. Can you walk in it? Some sheaths especially need to be tested for walking, as you don't want to waddle down the aisle.
5. Can you bend over in it? You may be hugging or lifting small children that day, so avoid the cleavage shot or a pinching bodice when you do bend.

Gown shopping smarts

The first piece of advice I'm going to give you is to go gown shopping by yourself at first. The idea is to choose the gown you like, without any pushy opinions or others' doubts as to the style. Remember, this is your wedding, and although it might be nice to share the experience with others, this first step is best taken on your own. Once you've chosen your gown— or narrowed your choices to two—then you can bring in your maid of honor for a selection session.

Never reject a dress for the way it appears on the hanger. Bride Karen Blake pulled what looked like a limp dress with strange pleats on the bodice out of a gown rack, and although her maid of honor wrinkled her nose and said no way, she tried it on. Sure enough, the bodice was perfect for her small frame, and the skirt was a great complement to the rest of her figure.

Always order just a little bit larger than you are. Sure, you have plans to lose weight for the wedding, but it might not happen. A seamstress can adequately take in a dress that's too big, but letting out a dress that's too small is complicated (and expensive) work.

Wear the same undergarments and shoes you'll wear on the wedding day so that you can get a better idea of the true fit of the gown. If your chest will be lifted higher with a strapless bra that gives good support, the gown will fit differently than with your standard strappy C-cup.

Never order a gown without trying it on first. This includes gowns you see on the Internet. Undoubtedly, you've heard a lot about Internet gown companies, companies that can copy celebrity gowns for a few hundred dollars, and designers who sell last season's wedding gowns online. Be wary of this, as some companies do not have return policies, alterations are not involved, you cannot truly see how the gown will work with your body shape and coloring, and you miss out on that wonderful service in the bridal salon.

Take good notes. If you'll be trying on several gowns at several stores, keep a written record of what you like where. Some shops won't give you the designer name of the gown, however. The labels have been ripped out of most gowns as a standard practice because so many brides were trying on gowns at stores, then calling the designer showroom or Internet wholesaler and getting the gown for less on their own. Shop owners have gotten smart, and they will not let you know whose gown you're wearing. Unfair, yes, but it's good business practice for the shop owners. As you take notes, write down a style number, explanations of the dress, and pricing and delivery information. You may choose to pull out the old Polaroid for a good comparison session later on, but that may not be necessary.

Examine the contract. Be sure all relevant information is in your contract, that delivery dates are set, refunds and cancellation clauses are written clearly, and any of your special requests are clearly defined. If alterations are free, be sure that is written in the contract as well, including the number of alteration sessions and the name of the seamstress you will be using.

Discuss delivery plans. The date of delivery should be several weeks before the wedding, but you should let the bridal shop owner know whether or not you'll be bringing the dress home or storing it at the shop. Since many marrying couples live together, brides often do not want the groom to see the dress before the wedding day. Or, they're afraid of damage to the dress. So specify the terms of dress storage at the shop. And get insurance for protection of your gown on their premises as well.

Renting gowns

Some brides are renting their wedding gowns. In some areas, wardrobe rental agencies carry wedding gowns, at prices as low as $200 to $300. The available dresses come right from designer trunk shows and discontinued style shows, and they are only rented three to four times before they are donated to a worthy cause.

Brides who have gone this route say that they loved the idea of renting their gown, as they are not the sentimental type, they wouldn't expect their daughter to wear any wedding gown of theirs, and they just didn't see the logic in spending $3,000 on a gown instead of on a honeymoon.

So if this option interests you, call around to wardrobe rental agencies and ask if they carry wedding gowns. Very often, they can refer you

to someone who does. Just research carefully, see the actual gown first and schedule fittings before the big day.

Fittings

Whether you're buying or renting your gown, whether you're getting a great dress off the rack at Macy's or wearing an antique dress you found in a shop at the beach, you will need to be sure your chosen dress fits you perfectly on the wedding day. That means alterations to your dress on several dates before the wedding.

No doubt you've gone through the alterations process before, so I won't give you the basic details that first-time brides need. But I will help you choose the best seamstress for the job:

- Get a seamstress recommendation from a recent bride in the area.
- If alterations are free at your bridal salon, ask to meet the seamstress ahead of time.
- Find out how busy the seamstress will be close to your wedding date.
- Visit the seamstress's workshop. Is it overloaded with back work? Unorganized? Are there endless messages on her answering machine?
- Interview the seamstress. See if she's kind and friendly, or if she just goes at the job saying nothing.
- Check out her fees.
- Establish a contract with her, stating the fitting dates, the price, delivery date, and delivery or pickup information.

Real brides share their stories

"I enjoyed trying on gowns SO much more this time around. My mother wasn't there, telling me that this gown would be so much better for my 'figure.' This time, it was just me, I knew what I wanted, and I found it in an enjoyable way."

—Samantha

"Compared to my first gown, this gown is just more me. The first gown looked like a cotton candy stick, and I battled with that blasted skirt all night. This time, I knew I wanted a simpler gown with a lower-cut neckline, a bit sexier, and I loved the reaction I got when I wore it to my wedding."

—Nancy

"After all that plastic surgery, you bet I was wearing a sheath dress this time around!"

—Marina

"I had two gowns—one more traditional A-line for the ceremony, and then I changed into a great, sexy pale blue dress with sparkles for the reception. Everyone said I'd never looked better, and the outfit change was an unexpected, dramatic touch."

—Fawn

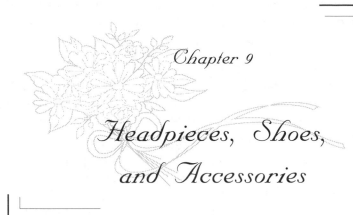

Chapter 9

Headpieces, Shoes, and Accessories

Your wedding look is not complete without the extras: a veil, a headpiece, a tiara, gloves, shoes, and anything else you choose to complement your gown and make you look gorgeous. Here, you'll learn about what the etiquette books say about veils for second-time brides, and you'll also find out what new trends exist on the market and in the fashion pages today.

Headpieces

A second-time bride has more of an option as to what she wants to wear on her head for the wedding. She isn't limited to the standard veil, and indeed there are rules about veils and encore weddings. Many options are open to you, as you'll see when you visit the bridal shops and flip through wedding magazines, so prepare yourself here to search for the styles that seem right to you.

Veils

The second-time bride *can* wear a veil, as long as it's an appropriate one. The blusher veil, the one that is worn over the face in the initial presentation of a first-time bride, is not allowed according to the rules of good taste, but a longer veil that hangs from the back of the head is perfectly fine.

You may choose a half-length veil, rather than a full-length one, as the lack of blusher veil means imbalance in the look. Most second-time brides go with a headpiece of some kind, with a half-length tulle veil attached for the bridal look without the throwback to the virginal wedding standard.

Tiaras

The tiara is a popular look right now, with many bridal designers showcasing their gowns and bridal fashions with the tiny, embellished headpieces serving as an anchor for a veil or as the sole accessory in the hair.

Tiaras come in all shapes and sizes now, and some are designed with a future in mind. For instance, the tiaras made with real pearls and gemstones by Winters and Rain (*www.wintersandrain.com*) can be worn on the wedding day as a bridal headpiece, and then the company will disassemble the tiara and create one or several separate pieces of jewelry from it. Your bridal headpiece can become a pearl necklace, a pearl and diamond pin, earrings, or a pendant perfect for your future collection or for handing down to your daughters as meaningful mementos.

The tiara design industry is booming, with pieces now available in genuine and faux jewels, intricately designed and lovely to look at. You can find tiaras to match the pearled trim of your gown or the glistening silver of your jewelry. Some even have miniature porcelain rosebuds to match your flowers or the floral accents on your dress.

The tiara is so popular now, it is outselling veils among second-time brides, who state that this particular headpiece makes them feel positively regal. It is the perfect accent to upswept hair, a completely new look for them, and a chance to be the belle of the ball. Tiaras can be worn with any style of wedding gown, from the sheath to the A-line to the ball gown, and even bridesmaids can be adorned with similar but less elaborate hairpieces to match.

Floral hairpieces

Especially for the more intimate, informal wedding, a delicate wreath of flowers can be worn over the bride's hair. This look too can be matched by the bridesmaids or the flower girls, and it gives a wonderful, natural look to the bridal style for an outdoor wedding.

If you don't like the ring of flowers sitting on your head, you might choose to have little wisps of flowers or baby's breath tucked into the sculpted twists of your upswept hairstyle. With the many options of bridal hair designs, such as multiple twists, rolls, chignons, French braids, and even loose, flowing curls, a good stylist can place floral accents in a lovely way. Practice this ahead of time with your stylist, bringing along a packet of real flowers or some inexpensive fake ones from the craft shop. This look needs to be perfected ahead of time so that the wedding day look is neither overdone nor a burden.

Other hair accents

Those accessory stores in the mall are not just for the 13-year-old set. There, you can find any number of jeweled hair clips, hairpins with tiny sculpted roses on them, rhinestone hair gems, and inexpensive simple headbands with gentle designs and accents. Very often, second-time brides do hit these stores for their sheer variety, for the lower prices (often under $20), and to avoid the higher expenses of real gem designs offered at department store counters or in bridal shops.

Another benefit, if you have a daughter, is to take her with you and let her help you pick out styles of headpieces for you, for herself, and for the bridesmaids. She'll love being the fashion coordinator in this instance, and you'll both share an enjoyable shopping trip.

Going without hair accents

Depending upon whether you will be wearing your hair up or down, you may not need any hair adornment at all. A loose, flowing ringlet style of hair is a relaxed, natural look for an informal gown and wedding setting. An elegant, upswept twist or sleek chignon is all the statement you may need.

In the bridal fashion magazines, and at weddings all across the country, brides are investing in the services of talented stylists who create veritable sculptures with their hair. The curls and well-placed tendrils are all the accent you need to bring the focus to your eyes, your face, your jewels, and the cut of your dress.

Your shoes

Of course, the key word here is comfort. You'll need to be sure that you choose shoes to complement your gown, heels that are the right height for you, and the right, broken-in fit to prevent aching feet and blisters.

Choose a simple style of shoe that does not compete with the design of the gown. Don't make the mistake of wearing a highly ornate shoe that is just too much. Most brides go with a simple 1/2" to 1" heel, so that they can walk comfortably and do not have to teeter down stairs.

One very important question you must ask yourself is "How do the shoes work with the wedding location?" This may seem odd, but you can learn from brides who regretted wearing tall, slender heels at a garden party, where their heels sank into the ground and they felt like they were wearing football cleats the whole day. Be sure your shoes are flat and provide good traction if you will be walking on cobblestone or on a slippery surface such as the deck of a boat. As far as shoes, the rule is: simplicity and comfort. Everyone will be looking at your face anyway. The shoes are just a smaller accent and a way to get you from place to place.

Of course you'll match the color of your shoes to your dress. Cream or ivory dresses call for cream or ivory shoes, and white matches white. You may choose to go with silver shoes if your gown is one of the popular shaded colors with silver threading and accents. Open up your options when selecting, knowing all the details of your gown to match in a complete look.

Shop for your shoes at the end of the day. Your feet swell during the day, particularly if you've been running around and quite active (as you will be on your wedding day) so try on shoes when your feet are the size they're likely to be on the wedding day. If they fit well in late afternoon, they should not be much of a bother during the wedding. Ill-fitting shoes are a complaint of many brides who wind up taking their expensive shoes off for most of the reception. Shop well now, and you'll avoid the pain and wasted money.

Buy your shoes way in advance. Wear them often to break them in, but be careful not to scuff them or get them marked in any way.

See the list of suggested shoe companies in the Resources section of this book. These shops specialize in bridal and bridal party shoes, and you may find a bargain and/or a wide selection of appropriate footwear for your entire bridal party, including the kids.

Other accessories

The wedding day look is not just made up of a gown, hair adornment, and shoes:

Jewelry

Again, depending upon the cut of your neckline and the style of your hair, your accessory choices are varied. Elaborate jewelry looks wonderful with upswept hair and a princess neckline, so consider dangling earrings and a flat spread of gems in your necklace.

Although most first-time brides go for the demure look, with pearl earrings and a pearl necklace, you are free to express your personal style and creativity with the type of jewelry you wish to wear with your gown. If your gown is colored, you may choose to wear jewels that accent that color. You may go with more dramatic diamond earrings, for instance, or a string of barely-there pink freshwater pearls with your blush pink gown. Accessory stores carry faux colored gemstone jewelry sets that may just suit your tastes and match the colors you'd like to highlight in your gown.

The options are up to you, and it is your choice as to whether to go bold with the accessories or to go for the simple, elegant look. Most brides I spoke to said that although they could cover themselves with diamonds, they still chose to keep the jewelry understated. A few simple pieces were just enough accent for them, and they wanted all the sparkle to be in their eyes.

Gloves

For a classic, elegant wedding, you might choose to wear long, elbow-length gloves. The look is reminiscent of the 1940s era and ballroom styles, and a bride in long gloves is a vision of sophistication. Glove designers now show their gloves in all colors and styles, simple or detailed, from white to cream to silver to dyeable to match gowns.

Do yourself a favor, though, and choose the type of glove that attaches at the middle finger and leaves your hands somewhat open for the slipping on of the ring and the better handling of champagne glasses, utensils, and the cutting of cake. Gloves designers know that brides need dexterity on the wedding day, and the best designs of gloves are those that allow the wearer to function as well as look elegant. Compare designs, try on the options, see how comfortable you are with the length of the glove, try them on with the gown, and make your decision based on feeling.

One warning about dyed gloves: don't do the dyeing yourself. One bride wanted light lavender gloves to match her gown and decided to save a few bucks by dyeing them herself in the washer machine. Although the gloves came out lovely for the wedding day, her arms retained a lavender hue for days afterward. If you must dye the gloves, get a professional to do it.

Chapter 10

Dressing the Bridal Party

Your bridesmaids and maid or matron of honor deserve to look and feel wonderful in their wedding day outfits as well, so you should certainly include them in the decision making process. In this section, you'll help your attendants choose the best gowns for them, ones they will definitely wear again. As a second-time bride, you may have learned from the first time around that your maids do not like being told what to wear, and as they are not inmates, they certainly should not be forced to wear a uniform.

Having "the talk" with your bridesmaids

Gather your bridesmaids together and discuss your vision for the wedding itself. They'll love hearing you share the many details, and they'll love seeing you glow as you anticipate the big day. At this time, you'll tell them about the formality of the wedding, the location, the style, and what you want as far as their wardrobes.

This is by no means a one-sided conversation. You ought to ask them what kind of dresses they want to wear according to the dictates of the formality of the wedding. Once they know they'll be in floor-length gowns, and you want them in forest green for your fall wedding theme, they'll be able to share with you what they prefer.

This discussion is best done out at a restaurant during lunch, or at your place for an informal brunch. Make it a celebration of your unity as a bridal party, and make the task a pleasant one. Bridesmaids do dread the unknown right before the gown choice is made for them, and yours will appreciate your respecting them enough to ask for their input.

One caveat, though: This can turn into a free-for-all if you do not set some parameters on the discussion and the gown choices. The maids will all want to look their best, but as they may be of all different ages, sizes, shapes, and tastes, they will certainly have their own votes for style of dress. Opening the decision up to them to make could be inviting a battle of wills and egos. You can control the discussion by beginning with a short speech saying you want to please them, and you understand that they want to look good, but there is only a small range of choices that you have for them. Then, pull out the three or four pictures that you've culled from bridal magazines, and see what the women have to say.

If you've chosen well, your maids may have no problem with the four options they have to consider. Many brides report that since their maids were older and wiser than the 21-year-old ones they had the first time around, they didn't negotiate so selfishly. These maids were willing to see the options as final, to avoid pushing and trying to be "the leader," and to negotiate well with the skills they've learned in the workplace and as more established adults.

Considering the bridesmaids' budget

One of the best things you can do is select gowns that fit your preferred tastes for the wedding party appearance, but with a great emphasis on the cost of the dress. You don't want to burden your maids with $3,000 gowns, and you don't want to financially punish them for agreeing to stand in your bridal party. The most beloved brides do take cost into consideration, remembering to add in monetary factors for alterations, shoes, accessories, travel, lodging, parties, and gifts. They are thoughtful of their maids' financial constraints, and they choose gowns based on value, not on designer name.

Considering the bridesmaids' shapes

A big mistake that first-time brides make is "assigning" a dress to their maids without any consideration of the women's differing sizes and shapes. In one bridal party, two of the more petite maids looked lovely in their suit dresses, but the two heavier ones looked bulkier (and miserable). Consider your maids' body shapes when thinking about gowns for them, and don't put them all in a style that some would never choose to wear on their own.

Think about your maids' shapes and how they dress as individuals. Follow the trend that's in place now, in which maids choose their own style of gown (as long as it fits with the formality of the wedding). The colors will all still match or be complementary if you order from the same designer's collection, and the maids will look lovely in styles that suit their shapes.

If one of your maids is pregnant, allow for her expanding size by asking her to choose the gown that she feel is best for her. Most pregnant bridesmaids go for A-line cuts—bought in a larger size to allow for growth over the coming months.

Again, your maids will love you for the freedom you give them, for allowing them to make their own decisions about their wedding-day wardrobe.

Ordering and fitting information

Once the styles are established at a group try-on session at the bridal salon, the seamstress must measure the maids. Remember that bridal fashions run small, and an 8 may not be an 8 that translates into a daily wardrobe. So the seamstress will measure the maids completely, and the order will be placed by those numbers.

This task should be highly organized, as ordering the maids' gowns can become complicated when some maids do not live in the immediate area. In the case of the distant bridesmaid, inform her of the style of gown either by sending her a picture or sending her to a Web site that shows an image of the gown. Instruct her to get her measurements taken on a standard sizing card at a legitimate seamstress's shop and to send the size card to you. Her gown will be ordered with the rest of the maids' gowns, so that the colors of the gowns will all match. It's well known in the fashion industry that gowns are made in different locations and that dye lots differ from place to place. A batch of hunter green gowns ordered in Philadelphia may clash with the hunter green gowns ordered in Phoenix, so place your order at one location.

Organizing the order

Be sure your bridesmaids' gown order is highly organized, and that each maid's full name and phone number is listed next to the size of her gown. Each maid will have to pay a deposit, and she will have to know when the final payment is due.

Find out when the gowns will come in, preferably six to eight weeks before the wedding, and have that promised delivery date written in the contract.

A good contract is of the utmost importance here, just as it is for the ordering of your gown, and the details of the alteration services must be spelled out as well. Be sure the shop writes down exactly how many fittings are included in the price of the order, what is free and what is extra, and whether or not extra embellishments are to be added to the gowns when they come in.

Get a signed copy of the contract, and keep it someplace safe. You will need it for your own organization and in case of delays and payment confusion. Assign the maid of honor to be in charge of collecting the payments from the maids.

This isn't a difficult task. It is just one that requires a great deal of diplomacy, organization, and focus. When the gowns come in, for instance, you may have to FedEx out a gown to the maid who lives far away for her fittings to be done in her area. Just keep on top of the multi-leveled aspects of this job, and know that you've already improved upon the way most women handle dressing their bridesmaids. Your consideration of their personal styles and budgets speaks volumes of your character.

Shoes and accessories for the bridesmaids

The same rules of comfort and fit that you've considered for your own wedding shoes apply to those of your maids as well. Be sure they will be in suitable shoes for the conditions of the wedding day, that they break their shoes in, and that they aren't expected to pay a fortune for designer styles.

Shoes for the bridal party should be ordered in one group, sent in as part of one dye lot, and paid for responsibly by the maids. Distribute the shoes to your maids ahead of time for breaking-in purposes, and at that time also give your maids several pairs of the color of stockings they'll be wearing on the wedding day. You'll want to have your maids in the same color pantyhose so that there is no noticeable color difference if their gowns are shorter. Choose sandal-toe styles if their shoes are open-toed. It's a great idea to do this at this time, so that they can keep their wedding-day stockings with their shoes until the day of the wedding.

Regarding dyeing shoes, you may opt against that choice. Many dresses go well with white, cream, or black shoes, especially if they will be hidden under long gowns, and the newest trend is wearing silver or copper-colored shoes that complement the gown and match the jewelry and hairpieces. So don't assume that shoe dyeing is the only option. See what those great silver sling-backs look like with the dress.

As far as accessories, your maids should wear similar styles of jewelry. They do not have to match exactly as your first set of bridesmaids did. Back then, you may have given your maids with the faux pearl necklaces and earrings they were to wear on the wedding day. Although you may choose to do that again for a lovely look, you may also choose to allow your maids to wear their own jewelry choices within a certain style range. For instance, you might ask your maids to wear a simple set of faux pearl earrings on the wedding day. That instruction keeps them from wearing what might be (in your eyes) their own gaudy preference for big gold hoop earrings, flashy nameplate necklaces, or rings on every finger. Just spell out your desires, and your maids should comply.

One nice trend now is matching purses. Bridesmaids do want to keep their wallets and lipsticks on them for their personal needs, and rather than have them all bring their everyday bags—or go out and get new bags— count a small beaded or decorated bag as part of their wedding wardrobe. Many new handbag designers are showcasing their wares on television, in the bridal magazines, and in standard women's magazines. Think of your maids' needs (and your own!) and get a set of matching handbags for the big day.

If your maids will be in gloves, schedule a trying-on session. Your maids will of course have different sized hands and arm lengths, so it may take a group try-on for you to see how full-length gloves will look on your bridal attendants. Some brides discover at this point that the differences in their maids' arms make for an odd look; on some maids the gloves are tighter and form-fitting, and on others, the gloves are droopy. Try on several different styles and sizes, and include open-fingered gloves in your search. Remind your maids that the gloves are only for the ceremony and that they will be free to remove them at the reception.

Your children in the bridal party

They may be your children, or they may be the flower girl and ring bearer that you've selected to be a part of your attendant group. This is where the wardrobe selection is a great deal of fun. Designers are putting lots of attention and detail into wedding attire for children of all ages, and the selections are as varied as those for bridesmaids' dresses. Some designers specialize in kids' special event clothing, and you may even find a children's dress to match your gown.

Older girls in the bridal party can choose their own style of dress in keeping with the bridal party colors, and for teenagers, this is often a fun shopping trip. They get to choose what they will wear on the big day, and with the assurance of getting plenty of attention, they often choose a beautiful gown that makes them feel like the bride themselves.

Younger girls can wear one of the many kids' fashion styles out there right now, and you may choose those from the bridal stores or even from regular kids' clothing stores. I've discovered lovely wedding-appropriate dresses in kids' discount clothing stores for $50 or less, and with an easily added sash or floral accent, these dresses can make the kids look adorable for your day.

The parents of child attendants will also appreciate your paying mind to budget, as some of the more upscale designer kids clothes can cost up to $500!

For kids' wedding wardrobes, simpler is almost always better, and they have a great chance of wearing the dresses again in the future. If you have children of your own, you know the value of getting multiple wearings out of any piece of clothing, so you can even allow the girls to wear a First Communion dress that has been fitted with a color-coordinated sash. There is no rule that says kids' clothing has to be new. It just has to be a fitting look for the day, and the kids have to be comfortable in the outfits chosen. If done well, your teenagers will glow and your smaller girls will twirl and perform for all your guests, feeling pretty in their party dresses.

About the men

The men need to be dressed well for the occasion too. In keeping with the rules of formality, your men might be outfitted in black tuxedoes with tails for an ultra formal wedding, black tuxes with black ties for a formal wedding, dark suits for a semi-formal wedding, or even khaki pants, white shirts and matching ties for an informal outdoor wedding. This last look is a wonderful one for garden weddings or beach gatherings, as your men look and feel comfortable in their group ensembles.

A tuxedo rental agent can help you choose the right tuxedo color, style, and fabric for the style and formality of your wedding, and again the men are subject to the rules of sizing cards and last-minute fittings. One thing to note is that the men's wedding fashion industry has expanded as well. No longer are you limited to a handful of tuxedo styles. Now, grooms and groomsmen are wearing smart-looking black tuxes with black shirts and black satin ties. They're adding color to their getups with colored thread, patterned vests, and even the type of boutonniere they wear. Men are far more fashion-conscious now than they used to be, and they do care about the outfit you're putting them in for the big day. So allow them some input, and do plenty of research on what they'll be expected to wear.

You'll choose the color of ties to match the bridal party, whether or not vests will be used, and the accessories such as cufflinks. Assign the best man the job of organizing the men in their ordering process, payment plans, and delivery.

One note about tuxedo rentals: Allow plenty of time before the wedding to search for the best styles and availability. If your wedding will be held in May or June, you will be competing not only with a great number of weddings, but also with proms. Be sure the company will have plenty of tuxedoes available at the time of your celebration, and that its styles reflect your tastes.

Real brides share their stories

"I asked my maids to pick out their pictures of the gowns they wanted to wear. They loved the color I had chosen, I loved the gowns they chose, and everything worked out fine. Of course, I only had three maids to deal with. This never would have worked if I'd had eight maids like last time."

—Vanessa

"We did the opposite of letting everyone wear their own style of dress. Instead, they agreed on a style, but then chose their own colors that went well with the color scheme of the wedding. So some were in blush pink, some were in more rose colors, some were in deeper pinks. We looked like a beautiful bouquet in the photos, and everyone was happy that they could wear the colors that suited their skin type."

—Maureen

"I just had flower girls as my attendants, and the girls were all in these pretty little dresses that I found at a discount shop for $39 each. They already had little yellow flowers on the bottoms, so it was perfect. I just added some yellow flowers to their floral headpieces, and the look was complete."

—Maryjane

"We had no idea what to do about the men's tuxes, so we brought pictures of our wedding site, pictures of the bridesmaids' gowns, and pictures of my gown to the tux manager. He pulled out some tuxedoes that went perfectly, and we chose from them. It saved us a lot of time, and the men looked great!"

—Angelica

"We had a big bridal party, so we negotiated the groom's tux for free since the men were all paying for their own tuxedoes. It was a great deal."

—Marsha

Chapter 11

The Rings

You know that the wedding rings are a symbol of your bond and eternal promises, but for you the selection is more about personal style and substance. According to Beth Reed Ramirez of *Bride Again*, second-time brides are spending more on their rings because they have more money to spend. Therefore, wedding ring selection is open to a wider variety of ring styles, more elaborate designs, and more precious metals and gemstones.

In addition, your ring selection is likely to be more of a statement of your personality. For your first wedding, you may have gone with a simpler, less expensive style of rings. You may have been sentimental and wanted the bride and groom rings to match. Your age and exposure may have limited your taste and knowledge of jewelry.

Now, you are more sophisticated, you have a better sense of yourself, and you know something about jewelry and what styles look best on your hand. Even better for you, the jewelry industry offers a much wider selection of wedding bands and rings than it did just 10 years ago. Different metals are in style, different designs are available, and there are more designers to choose from.

In this section, you'll explore your own wedding band shopping tastes, you'll learn about the newest trends in rings, and you'll also consider bonding rings for your children.

Wedding ring trends

The wedding ring industry is enormous and varied now, as brides and grooms have developed more of a sense of personal style with regard to jewelry. Perhaps it is the influence of the celebrity world and fashion magazines, or the increased coverage of jewelry at big celebrity events such as the Academy Awards and Golden Globes, that affects "regular" people's choices in wedding ring designs.

You may still see and choose the simple, plain, unadorned wedding band styles of yesteryear, but now you have a choice of patterned, dual-metal, lacy cut, and gemstone rings. This explosion of styles is a wonderful surprise to many brides, as they intend to find wedding rings that are different from the first rings they wore. Virtually all of the brides I spoke to said they wanted more elaborate rings, rings that were more "them," and rings that matched the value they put upon themselves. They wanted more choice over the rings they selected, and their increased ring budget allowed them to choose whatever they wanted.

Remember that the *Bride Again* survey reported that the average second-time bride is spending between $2,500 and $5,000 on wedding rings. That's a far cry from what you might have spent on your first rings, and it allows you to consider whole new worlds of ring designs.

What's hot in the market

Right now, platinum is the most popular choice of wedding bands. Gold and gold-coated choices are still around, but the big emphasis is on the more durable metallic qualities of platinum and the look of silver against the sparkle of diamond. Ramirez says that this surge in popularity is due to "the increases in technological advances in platinum, whereby the jewelry designers are finding that particular metal easier to work with and design." You'll find patterned styles, lacy cuts, gilt edges, and matte shades of the metal in rings of all designs.

Platinum, as you'll see with jaw-dropping regularity no matter where you look, is more expensive than gold, but the price reflects the metal's durability and the design and value of the rings themselves.

Bridal advertising, fashion magazines, Web sites, and ring shops are showing a great variety of ring styles, distancing themselves from the traditional styles and bowing to the more upscale design wishes of the average shopper. Today's bride is more savvy about jewelry design, and the market is well aware of her exposure to advertised styles and her willingness to spend more on the ring of her dreams.

For instance, you will find grooved bands, and laurel leaf designs from Cathy Waterman. Tiffany and Co. offers rounded platinum bands set with diamonds. Double-metal designs offer eye-catching and outfit-coordinating mixes of platinum and gold. The options are endless, as you will see while you're flipping through catalogs or walking the long, brightly lit design cases in jewelry stores.

It's not just diamonds anymore

You've seen plenty of wedding bands with diamond accents to match the engagement ring. It's been a trend even for first-time brides for decades, and these adorned rings are still a large part of the jewelry industry. Now, though, designers recognize that the large number of second-time brides who happily break from tradition want more personalized rings. So you may see more wedding bands set with gemstones other than diamonds. Three set emeralds are extremely popular now, as are rubies and sapphires. Birthstones set in platinum are on the rise, providing the ultimate statement of individuality and personality.

The groom's wedding band

Just like the bride's wedding band options, the groom's options are quite diverse. Today's man may choose a simple gold band, or he may go with a patterned band. Today's designers acknowledge men's sense of style as well, offering a wide selection of designs, including platinum inlaid with gold, additional dual metals, and matte finishes. Men like their rings to coordinate with their watches, so a dual metal ring will match a silver or gold watch quite nicely.

They don't have to match

Today's couples see themselves as individuals who are joining together. They are more independent, have a better sense of personal style, and are more willing to make their own choices. So in the wedding industry, we are seeing fewer matching wedding band sets and more individual selections. The bride may choose a lacy cut platinum band to match her more romantic side, and the groom may go with a simpler band to match his personality. So do not be swayed by the sentimentality of matching styles, even if the twin set may be slightly less expensive than separate styles. You are choosing rings you'll wear forever, and you'll want the choice to be yours.

Engraving

You may choose to have your rings engraved, either on the inside or on the outside. That choice may come as a surprise to you, as you may think the engravings are only for the inside of the ring. But designers are showing outside engravings now, such as single words like "Love" and "Eternity." You may see Latin and other languages engraved on the outside of rings as well.

Still, the most common practice by far is the inside engraving of rings, such as your names, your wedding date, "I Love You," or "I Will Love You Forever." Some couples choose to engrave their nicknames, the date they met, or the title of their wedding song. The choice is up to you, and it is a special addition to any wedding ring.

Design your own rings

With your maturity and wisdom comes a great sense of your own style. So you may choose to create your own design of wedding bands. This practice brings a tremendous amount of personal meaning to the traditional symbol of your marriage, and at the very least it allows your creativity to shine as brightly as your diamonds.

The easiest way for you to accomplish this is through the Web site *www.adiamondisforever.com*, which offers a ring design site that allows you to try out 7,500 different styles, shapes, gemstones, and metals. You can then print out your personalized design and bring it to a custom jeweler for the best creation of your rings. You can also download the image and e-mail it to any person you'd like to see your artistic work.

Some couples check out this site and have great fun designing rings that they know they'll never have made. It is a bonding experience that many brides report has brought some fun into the planning experience, a little diversion from the shopping and planning, and an enjoyable sense of play to the process. One groom designed the ring he wished he could afford for his bride, and he saved it with a promise to deliver that style on their 10th wedding anniversary. The bride loved the gesture, and even if he doesn't deliver at year 10, his efforts and intentions warmed her heart and further solidified their love for one another.

Rings for the children and as a new family

If you have children, you might choose to follow the example of other couples who have bought gemstone rings for their kids to wear. For some, an amethyst or emerald ring is the first valuable gemstone ring the child has ever owned, and it is a symbolic gift that means a commitment to a "priceless" family member.

You might also choose to have a "mother's ring" made in addition to the kids' individual gemstone rings. The "mother's ring," as I'm sure you've seen, is a simpler band of gold, platinum, or sterling silver that incorporates all of the birthstones of all of her children. As your two families combine into one, perhaps you and the kids can wear variations on the all-inclusive gemstone rings or pendants that symbolize the quality and preciousness of your family members.

Ring shopping advice

As with all other aspects of planning your wedding, you will need to concern yourself with the quality of the vendor you select for this big investment. Your wedding ring is an important purchase, and the monetary involvement is a big one. Choose a jeweler that you have known for years, one who has established a long-standing positive reputation in your area. Your jeweler should be a true professional with great knowledge of the ring industry, not just some salesman who has to look everything up in a book.

Be sure your rings are of high quality. Precious metals should be stamped with an indication of their quality, such as 24k for 24 karat, PT for platinum, and so on. The diamonds or gemstones you choose should be rated according to their class and category. (If you need a reminder about choosing quality diamonds, as in the 4Cs of color, cut, clarity, and carat, visit *www.adiamondisforever.com*) Ask as many questions as you see fit, and choose a jeweler who is patient with you.

A good jeweler will discuss the options, tell you which styles look good on your hand, and explain the realities of maintaining and protecting the precious metals you've chosen. One bride spoke highly of her jeweler, sharing with me the story of how he suggested titanium bands for their strength, lightness, and color variation. She wanted something a little different, and she hadn't found anything she liked yet. The jeweler led her to the titanium bands, and she found exactly what she wanted. A good jeweler will be concerned about what you want, not with making the big sale.

Order "comfort fit" rings, which have a smooth edging of metal that allows for a more smooth fit of the ring. While sizing and re-banding can be done at a later date, the initial trying-on period should include some thought as to the functionality and fit of the ring and not just the sparkle of the diamonds or the shine of the metal.

Think also of what your ring will face while it's on your finger. If you do a lot of hands-on work, you may not want to choose a ring that can be scratched or suffer the loss of diamonds. Think about grooved or engraved rings' tendency to collect dirt or other foreign materials in the details, and what it will take to clean out the fine details of the ring on a regular basis. Your ring selection should take into account what your lifestyle is like so that you do not have to spend the rest of your life worried about damaging your precious jewelry.

When ordering the rings of your choice, do *not* just tell the jeweler what size you wear. As in wedding gowns, sizes may vary slightly with different designers, and you may not be aware of what your true ring size is. Over time, your ring size may change, such as after a pregnancy, weight loss, weight gain, or simple growth or aging. Even if the rings you own slip into a groove on your finger, it is important to order this ring in your true ring size. So allow your jeweler to measure your finger for your true size, and order accordingly.

Remember to get all details written in your ordering contract, including the style and size of your rings, the price, information on sizing, engraving, and cleaning, the delivery date, exchange information, refund information, and all other pertinent data. Of course, always get insurance for your rings, and have them appraised at a site other than the one at which you bought them.

Chapter 12

Flowers

This is the one area of wedding planning that affords you the most freedom and enjoyment. You are not very restricted by the rules of formality and what's acceptable; only your budget and your imagination limit you. Flowers are a part of virtually every wedding, and they have been since the beginning of time. You undoubtedly have some vision as to your floral design, from your bouquets to your centerpieces to floral arches and the rose petals your flower girls will scatter to sweeten your path.

In this section, you'll consider your vision for the flowers for your wedding, and you'll learn how to work with today's floral industry to bring your visions to beautiful and fragrant fruition. Again, much has changed in the wedding industry over the past years, and you may be surprised by the personalized attention you'll receive from any floral designer. You will be delighted at your sense of freedom, your partnership with a designer, and the new options in flowers and greenery that are presented to you.

So ready yourself for an enjoyable foray into the world of natural beauty. This is an exciting and uplifting job, one that gives most brides the greatest sense of creativity and expression. Choosing your flowers for your wedding is like painting a picture, and you are the creator of a work of art.

Where to start

Having been through this before, you know the basics of ordering flowers for your wedding. You know what is involved in the selection process, meeting with a floral designer, choosing the flowers you want, placing an order, and seeing the final picture on the wedding day. What's new to you now are two things: Your style has changed and floral industry trends have changed. The best way to start your flower shopping process is to take time to think about what you want, which again is a reflection of who you are.

What do you want?

Now, as compared to your first wedding, you may have favorite flowers. Daisies may be your signature bloom, or perhaps calla lilies are. You do not have to feel limited to the traditional white roses and stephanotis. You may want color in your bouquet, perhaps pastel or perhaps a vibrant hue. You may want all of your flowers to be the same style, or you may want a great variety of flowers and expressive centerpieces that are more your style.

Begin by thinking about what you picture for your day. This takes into account the style of wedding you want, and even the season. If you'll be having an informal wedding in April, will you want small bunches of low-cut tulips in rounded bowls as your centerpieces? If your wedding will be a beach wedding, will you want such exotic flowers as birds of paradise? For a romantic outside garden wedding or a formal wedding at a mansion, will you want romantic calla lilies and pale pink roses? Examine your vision, know what you want, and be able to describe it to your floral designer.

A very good idea is to scour wedding magazines for images of wedding flowers. If you can bring photos to your designer, it will be easier for her to create what you want, or to create a variation according to your wishes.

One factor that is going to determine your floral picture is the time of year. As you well know, certain flowers are in season at certain times of the year, and they are as such appropriate for weddings of that time. An efficient way for you to figure out what's best for your wedding season is to visit your floral designer during the same season of your wedding, a year before your wedding date. This way, you can see what types of blooms are in. If your planning schedule does not permit for this luxury, consider the sample seasonal list below:

Spring: Daffodils, tulips, hydrangeas, peonies, irises.

Summer: Roses, daisies, gerbera daisies, lilies, dahlias, sunflowers.

Autumn: Chrysanthemums, apple blossoms, asters.

Winter: Roses, evergreens, holly.

Your florist should be able to show you a chart of which types of flowers are in season, which are grown domestically, which are imported, and which are among the most economical choices.

The trends in the floral industry

As a second-time bride, you are not as bound by the rules of tradition or by what other people want for your wedding. What others are doing may not be so important to you, but you should be aware of what is going on in the floral industry so that at the very least you know your options.

Angela Lanzafame of The Potted Geranium in East Hanover, New Jersey says that all of the floral arrangements that brides are ordering are smaller. Those big, overbearing centerpieces that no one can see past are out of the picture, as are the long, flowing, heavy bouquets that hide the bride's gown and strain her arms during her walk down the aisle.

Everything from the bouquets to the centerpieces may be smaller in size, but they are by no means less impressive. Beautiful, top-quality flowers are arranged in tight bunches, either in the popular, rounded Biedermeyer style, nosegays, or even the hanging pomander style, which is very in for second-time brides right now. In all cases, smaller is better, as the bride is the focus of the day.

In most cases, says Lanzafame, the floral budget is larger for second-weddings, which allows the bride and groom to choose a better selection of the floral arrangements they want. They can afford the more exotic, imported blooms, and they can afford more detail to the design of their vision. If you are limited by budget, however, this doesn't mean that you are left out of the fun. A good floral designer will help you create a four-figure floral picture for much less, with the right decisions and artistry. All options are open to you if you shop well, design well, and make good use of the industry's trends.

As you will see during your investigation period, flowers are available in all budget ranges, so that makes for great customization options. You can have whichever flowers you want, in the design that you want, and you may even discover new styles that you've never heard of before.

Certain flowers are among the most popular for weddings right now, says Marilyn Waga of the esteemed floral design studio Belle Fleur in New York City. "We're using more roses, calla lilies, hydrangeas, and fragrant lilacs," she notes. Waga says that brides are using more color in their floral arrangements, reflecting their own hued gowns, their bridal parties' gowns, and even the seasons of their weddings. For instance, a bride planning a fall wedding may choose apple blossoms. For a spring wedding, she may opt for cherry blossoms. In the spring and early summer, a peak time for weddings, most floral designers receive requests for peonies arranged in clear glass bowls.

"We're seeing fewer over-the-top choices," says Waga. "Brides are selecting less wedding-ish floral designs, brighter colors, and making good use of what's available and seasonal." Waga also reports that the general wedding look in flowers is more subtle and understated, yet sophisticated and upscale—probably like yourself.

Tips for your flower order

* Be sure your flowers enhance your gown, not hide it.
* Go with smaller bouquets for your maids. Simple nosegays are popular now.
* Get special nosegays or floral baskets for your kids.
* Even if your parents are not paying for the wedding, it's a nice gesture to give them corsages and boutonnieres anyway.
* Do not be reined in by tradition. Exercise your creativity with all floral orders.
* Order flowers for your wedding cake. Your florist can tell you which blooms are safe to use, and even which are edible!
* To save money, don't select the cheapest flowers you can find. Instead, order fewer high quality, beautiful flowers and use more greenery. Your florist will be skilled at making less look like more, and your floral pieces will look far pricier than they actually are.

Other items from the floral designer

The best floral designers offer not only rose-strewn bouquets and centerpieces, but a variety of other items as well. Ask yours about floral arches, flowers and greenery to decorate your chuppah, ring bearer pillows, and fabric swags and tulle for encasing your rented chairs. You may even be able to purchase flowers and other items wholesale for making favors.

You might be surprised at what a good floral artist or wedding coordinator can accomplish. Topiaries can adorn tabletops and windowsills, and baskets filled with fruits, flowers, moss, and greenery can serve as ambience enhancing centerpieces. Consider large glass bowls filled with water, floating candles, and slices of lemon, lime, or kiwi for a natural and aromatic look that goes with today's wedding colors.

Check out the pricing of candles, which come in all colors and sizes, and which can be encrusted with sparkling rhinestones or embedded with seashells and other items. Floral managers can also provide aisle runners and pew decorations that depart from the usual tulle bow and roses. Always ask what the florist can provide, and compare the prices and quality to that offered by the rental agency you choose.

Placing your flower order

After you've chosen your florist, considered your options, and created your floral vision, it's time to place your flower order. You'll find a flower order checklist in Appendix I to keep you organized and to help make sure that your flower order is complete.

As with all wedding arrangements, be sure to have a complete contract filled out, with an itemized list of all purchases. Especially important are delivery instructions, as certain items within your order will be delivered to different sites. Again, insert a "time is of the essence" clause to be sure your flowers will arrive when they're supposed to, and keep careful track of payment schedules.

Floral centerpiece alternatives

I've left this for last, as it might be a wise idea to consider skipping the traditional floral centerpieces. Although the trend in floral centerpieces is now to have smaller, tightly clustered bunches of peonies, tulips, roses, or other flowers, the price tag is still high for each one. If your budget is better spent on the menu or your gown, you might consider skipping the pretty floral centerpieces in favor of non-flower items.

Candles are a popular option today, as many brides are choosing white or pale hued pillar candles of varying heights with rose petals sprinkled on the table around the base. The look of flickering candles around the room is a lovely, romantic option compared to the traditional look of floral pieces of yesteryear.

Fruit sculptures are not just fruit baskets, but elegantly arranged stacks of fruit in pretty glass bowls. No dye lot does as wonderful a job of producing lovely hues as Mother Nature, and you may find that a bowl of ripe pears matches your maids' gowns exactly. Consider pale lemons, green apples, or collections of exotic fruits such as starfruit and kiwi, papayas, mangoes, and plantains.

Bread baskets. Yes, you've seen simple bread baskets on your table at a restaurant, but your centerpiece may be an overflowing collection of

Italian rolls, marble rye, pumpernickel, grissini, and other mouthwatering breads. Have your caterer provide a selection of spreads such as garlic butter, spiced butters, whipped vegetable cream cheese, virgin olive oil, or tapenade. Your guests will love digging into your centerpiece!

A bowl of seashells. For a beach-theme wedding, nothing is easier or less expensive than a glass bowl filled with some sand and a collection of seashells. Craft stores carry bags of shells for just a few dollars, and in my personal opinion a starfish should be included in each one. To illustrate why, allow me to share this story with you:

After a divorce or the death of a spouse, it can feel as if a part of you has been ripped away. In my own healing, I read Anne Morrow Lindbergh's *Gift From the Sea*, in which she writes about how a starfish re-grows an arm if that arm is torn off. It regenerates. Lindbergh goes on to compare that to how that part of us that is ripped away does grow back, and sometimes stronger than before.

As you prepare to marry again, regardless of the type of loss you suffered after your first marriage, you or that hurt part of you has grown back stronger than before. Incorporating a starfish into your beach theme is a way to acknowledge your return to wholeness.

Topiaries. Okay, I have no dramatic story for this, but topiaries are a lovely idea for a garden wedding.

Collections of framed photos. Nothing will get your guests mingling more than the display of family wedding pictures and lovely shots of the two of you.

Display of favors. If you've wrapped your favors, the wrapped gifts can be stacked attractively.

A simple candelabra. For an elegant look, a polished silver candelabra can provide romantic lighting and ambience.

These are just some of the ideas to choose from. If you will have a theme wedding, your centerpiece may reflect your theme. If you will have a child's table, you might supply coloring books and small, *quiet,* hand-held computer games to occupy the kids' time and attention. The options are up to your creativity and budget, and to the vision you have for your wedding day.

Chapter 13

Invitations

T he invitation world is one that does require you to adhere to some standard etiquette. Although an invitation is simply the conveyance of the time and date of your wedding for your guests' knowledge, a great deal more information is contained within it. Moreover, the rules of etiquette and formality do still apply to the wording of your invitations and other printed items.

Because you already know how to order, address, and assemble invitations, I will address some of the new issues that you will have to deal with. We will skip the true basics, but I must delve into the mechanics a bit in order to help you create a suitable invitation package and a functional stationery set.

Your invitation's hidden messages

You know that the invitation provides your guests with the date, time, and place of your wedding, plus the location and time of your reception. But you may not be aware that a second-time wedding invitation has a *greater* responsibility than a first-time invitation in that it has to accurately convey the formality of the wedding to your guests. I just received a lovely invitation for my cousin's second wedding. It was a gorgeous invitation of off-white, with pale hunter green hearts and matching print. It gave the date and time of her home wedding, which I am personally aware will be in her backyard. However (and the rest of the family called me with the same question), I had no idea what the formality was. It was a three o'clock wedding, but was the dinner a formal one, or an informal one? At that hour, it could be anything. None of the guests, including myself, knew what to expect, and our biggest concern was how to dress. Some planned on long skirts, some planned on short skirts with a sweater for the possibility of a cool evening. Some bought formal dresses, and others questioned that move in favor of wearing a more businesslike outfit.

Why did we not get the message? It was all in the wording. Some of the invitation was worded formally, and other sections were informal. So remember, your entire invitation package has to express the formality of the event, so that the guests know what to wear.

Your wording not only conveys a dress code, it also gives your guests an idea of what to expect for the wedding itself. If your invitation states that your ceremony will be held at a church and your reception at home, then the guests know that they'll have to arrange for some extra transportation in the middle of the day.

Your wording, as you'll see later in the chapter, also indicates which members of the recipient's family are invited, and what other options they need to know for their plans to attend your wedding.

Invitation styles

If you've seen those stacks of thick invitation catalogs in card stores, you know that there are millions of designs and styles of wedding invitations on the market right now. Add to that the thousands available in the newer mail order catalogs and online invitation companies, and the available options are even more diverse than those found in the gown and floral worlds combined. Wedding invitations are a form of artistry, and because there are so many variations on wedding ceremonies and styles, the invitations market reflects an entire universe full of options for you to choose from.

Of course, the trend within the industry for first-time brides is still the simple, classic, unadorned ecru invitation with the correct wording and the correct amount of detail. You, however, are free to select a more creative style, depending upon the wedding you've planned and your personal style. Some brides take full advantage of the fact that they can have the colored trim this time, along with the detailed images and artwork on the invitation cover, and some are sticking with the elegant simplicity of a formal no-nonsense design.

The invitation design staffers at Siegel's, in Madison, New Jersey, say that second-time brides in their upscale area are ordering traditional wedding styles in ecru or very pale blush colors, and there may be some color to the wording. But by far, the majority still adhere to cream-colored with black lettering. Designs are not too fancy or ornate, they say, and brides are staying far away from cutesy cherubs and glitter.

The new invitation options

In recent years, you may have seen some articles and announcements about e-mail invitations. Although a few brides and grooms may have tried this high-tech option, it is by no means recommended for you. Some of the brides and guests I spoke to said that even if e-mailed invitations made the task easier and less expensive, the final outcome was a nightmare.

As computer systems and e-mail carriers are not infallible, some guests did not receive their e-mailed invitations. Some people's systems only delivered part of the message, and some older guests who only dabbled in computer usage and who did not check their e-mail never received the invitations at all. Some guests who did receive e-mailed invitations (lovely and personalized as they were) complained afterwards about downloading and printing problems. The overwhelming response was that e-mailed invitations were tacky and impersonal and made the bride and groom look lazy. So do not consider anything other than paper invitations, no matter what style you choose.

Wording of invitations

You're aware by now that the wording of invitations is highly important. Using "favour" and "honour" in place of "favor" and "honor" conveys an announcement of ultra-formality of the wedding style, and it tells your guests that they can expect a formal wedding. A more informal style of announcing the wedding tells your guests that they can expect a more laid-back reception. Consider the following:

You are invited to kick off your shoes
And take in some sun
At the oceanside wedding
of
Melina and Tom
Saturday, May 29
At 2:00pm
Johnson's Beach
Bring your sunscreen and join us
For an afternoon of Mai Tais
And an evening clambake by the fire.

Melina and Tom's invitation wording told their guests to expect a fun, casual, day-and-night wedding at the beach. With this announcement, the guests knew the weather conditions they'd face and their wardrobe options. Best of all, the couple's enthusiasm for the event shone through the wording, not just the style, of the invitation.

There is simply not enough room here for me to instruct you about the wording of an invitation for a semi-formal wedding at an arboretum or a wine-tasting party. The sample books and catalogs you check will give you plenty of options for wording instructions according to the style of your wedding. Also, your invitations ordering expert can advise you personally of the best wording choices.

Who's doing the announcing?

For your first wedding, you may have had to go the traditional route and put your parents' names first as the announcers of the wedding. Etiquette books contain all of the various wording variations to fit individual family situations—divorced parents hosting, one divorced parent hosting, mother and stepfather hosting, widowed parent hosting, and so on. For your second wedding, it is most likely that you, as the couple, are hosting your own wedding. This way, you do not have to bother with the family dynamics headaches that some couples have to deal with. It can be just your names, as simple as: "Melina Desideras and Tom Hendricks invite you to join them at...."

Another popular option for couples who have children is to have the kids do the announcing. Beth Reed Ramirez of *Bride Again* suggests this wonderful idea as a way to make the children an important part of the day.

Not only will the kids love being the "hosts," and knowing that their "blessing" comes through on the invitations, but your guests will enjoy the originality and the meaning of the attribution. Just be sure to check with the kids and see if it's okay to make that decision. Some couples wrongly print such an announcement only to give their guests the impression that the kids are fine with the union, when in fact the kids are quite bitter about it. Having kids announce the wedding on the invitations is a great idea if it expresses their true feelings.

Ordering invitations

Ordering invitations is not only a matter of getting the correct wording in addition to the right style for your tastes and suitability for the wedding. It is a detailed task that requires some special attention.

Enclosures

When you choose an invitation style, you will have the option of enclosure items that you want to include with the invitation. Most wedding invitations, no matter what the formality level, do include the following:

- ❧ Response cards.
- ❧ Reception cards.
- ❧ Maps to the ceremony and reception.

Some people also include hotel information cards, which is a great way to avoid having to take hundreds of phone calls to let your guests know about the best hotels in the area. Simply provide a list of hotels and a quote of their nightly prices, as well as some information about the hotels. The best hotel information cards inform guests about the hotel's amenities, such as pools, saunas, Jacuzzis, health clubs, and restaurants. This one step will help your guests make their own hotel reservations, if you have not simply given them information about the block of rooms you've reserved at one particular place.

The ordering process

Once you have the style numbers for your invitations and all manner of enclosures, you are ready to order your invitations. Most brides order too many, because they go by their guest headcount. But when you consider that your guests may come as couples or families, you'll see that several people's names are included on one invitation. So spend some time looking at your guest list, figure out how many invitations you'll actually need (remembering that single people over 16 get their own invitations), and order 20 percent more than that figure. Why 20 percent more? It leaves room for extras in case any negative responses from guests allow you to invite additional people from your "maybe" list. It allows for keepsakes that can be framed or mounted onto a celebratory candle. Having extras is fine; it's not having enough that is the problem.

If you'll be ordering from a card store or catalog, fill out the inscription section carefully, using the most precise handwriting you can. If ordering over the phone, which does happen when couples order through the new and highly praised catalog companies, enunciate and spell each difficult word or name. That is something I suggest to all brides. Have the order-taker read the invitation back to you, and have her spell the words out as she has written them. That prevents printing errors, extra expense, and stress.

Pay with a credit card, of course, and get a good contract, including delivery date, cancellation notice, and refund information. Different companies deliver in different amounts of time, and some will rush your order and send it to you via overnight delivery. Consider your time needs, and remember that your invitations have to be mailed at least eight weeks prior to the wedding. Allow 12 weeks if you will be asking guests to make extensive travel plans to be at your wedding, or if your wedding will be held during a popular vacation season.

Do-it-yourself invitations

Many second-timers get very involved in customizing their weddings. This might include designing and printing your own invitations. With computer graphic programs, word processors, color printers, and scanners easily accessible, many couples are saving money and sharing memories by creating their own invitations.

If this option is for you, spend some time looking through clip art or finding the best graphics or borders for your invitations, and search through the wedding paper stock in office supply stores. During one visit to a popular office supply store in my own area, I saw a great variety of wedding papers with lovely designs on them, for just under $15 per pack. These papers, available in a variety of weights and hues, make designing your own invitations easier. The spelling is up to you, the wording is up to you, and you can play with the design up until the last minute. Best of all, it is a far less expensive option.

If you plan to design your own invitation but still want the highest paper quality, take a copy of your design to a local printer and order the number of copies you need on one of the available paper types. Paper too has come a long way over the years, with recycled or patterned papers on shelves now. So look through a sample book, feel the grain of the paper, see what the print looks like on that paper, and have a professional do the job for you. Very often, printers can deliver your order in just a few days.

As far as envelopes, order 25 percent more than you think you'll need, as there isn't a bride alive who hasn't made some sort of spelling or addressing error while filling out her envelopes. Extras can be used for other tasks.

Using "Love" stamps for the inner and outer envelopes is status quo in the industry, but some brides are taking their individual themes right to the stamps they affix. Check with your post office about the availability of different stamp designs. Some couples who choose to have a beach-theme wedding can get stamps with an appropriate image on them. For a garden wedding, there are plenty of stamps with flowers of all varieties. One couple who held their wedding at Disney World used Disney stamps.

Wedding programs

Over the years, providing guests with wedding programs has become the norm rather than the exception. Guests love knowing what's coming up next in the ceremony, and if yours will depart from the usual they may appreciate any explanations of rituals or a lineup of events.

At one traditional Ukrainian wedding, the bride and groom included in their programs a printed explanation of what the elements of their ceremony meant. For example, their ethnic tradition stipulated the involvement of a sponsor couple who had been married a long time and who would take on the responsibility of mentoring the marrying couple. The program also explained Ukrainian words to the guests, who enjoyed being able to follow along.

Your program may not have to serve as a translation pamphlet, but it should outline all the steps of your ceremony as you have planned it. Other items to include, in whatever design you choose, are:

- The date and time of your wedding.
- The "hosts" of your wedding, if they are your children.
- The elements of your ceremony, from moment one to the recessional.
- The names of readers and performers.
- The names of the members of your bridal party.
- A personal message from the two of you.
- These are the usual elements of the standard program. Recent brides have also included:
- An explanation of who the bridal party members are.
- A special tribute to the people who introduced them.
- A copy of their vows.
- Their home address.
- An announcement of the bride's name change, if applicable.
- A tribute to departed family members.
- Poetry.
- Pictures of the couple alone or with their children.

Wedding programs today are coming in great varieties of styles. Covers are glossy and feature lovely images and works of art. Natural fiber paper is tied with elegant ribbon. Beautiful decorative print accents the wording. Program folders even contain packets of flower seeds for the guests to plant in the couple's honor.

The choices are endless, and most brides report that this task was a fun one for the couple to do together as a team. Grooms say that the program was one of the places where it was most comfortable for them to express their individuality, and they loved the feedback they received from guests. You will too, when you hold the final product in your hand.

Chapter 14

Showers and Registries

Yes, you can have a wedding shower! The old rules, which say a second-time bride cannot have a shower because it's a shameless plug for gifts, are a thing of the past. According to *Bride Again* magazine's annual survey, a full 68 percent of second-time brides register for gifts. Of those, half register at more than one place, with department stores, specialty stores, home refurbishing stores, and a host of online stores leading the list. Today's second-time bride is allowed to have a shower, so "help" your bridal party become aware of that fact.

Can you call it a shower?

While some bridal parties do still send out the standard "Showers of Happiness" cards to all the invited guests, many second-timers are more comfortable being the guest of honor at a non-titled brunch or dinner. As the wedding industry itself is not so caught up in titles and rules, neither are the parties given for you. Although the decision is not up to you—as no one should demand a shower, plan one for herself, or instruct the maid of honor as to what to call it—you can subtly express your wishes about whether or not you'll be receptive to a shower. Your honor attendant should know you well enough to judge whether or not you would be irked by the word "shower."

The popularity of second-time showers

Most second-time brides want a bridal shower. Most of the women I've spoken to said they wanted the whole wedding experience. They didn't want anything left out, and not having a shower of some sort would be a glaring omission to their total wedding experience.

"They also want to avoid guesswork when it comes to gifts," says Beth Reed Ramirez of *Bride Again*. Second-time brides may not need pots and pans, as they likely have all of the housewares they need, but they will appreciate other types of gifts that they are far more likely to use. That is one of the best advantages of being a second-time bride. You know what you want this time. The things you registered for the first time have probably been sold at a garage sale long ago, and you found that you had to use your wedding money to get the items you really needed. Now, you have the basics—the vacuum, air purifier, the great cutting knives. You know you don't need the lemon zester, the apple peeler, and the popcorn maker. Second-time brides have a greater sense of who they are, and they have a greater sense of the things they need, rather than the things they want.

Another issue related to this one is that guests don't want to guess either! They *want* to have a registry to go by. They *want* to give a good gift at the shower or the wedding. They don't want to get you a duplicate gift or something that doesn't fit who you are right now. So registering and having a shower is completely acceptable in today's wedding world, both for your sake and for your guests'.

Kinds of showers

Showers for all brides are no longer the usual everything-for-the-kitchen types of affairs. As most brides marry later in life now, and we're not seeing as many 21-year-old brides who are setting up a first home with these gifts, showers are taking on a new look. Even first-time brides are now registering at places like Home Depot and wineries, hoping for gifts they can really use to build a life and to reflect their interests. The woman of today may need cutting boards or bread-baking machines, but that's not all she's about.

As a second-time bride, you have the luxury of choosing a shower theme. In fact, theme showers are most popular for the more mature and established bride and groom, as they give the couple what they want and the guests a good focus on what to buy for them. Here are some shower theme ideas in case your bridal party asks what your biggest needs are:

- Lingerie showers.
- Music showers.
- Art showers.
- Gardening or home repair showers.
- Book showers.
- Wine showers.
- "Gag gift" showers.

Unfortunately, you still can't have a money shower, even if you'd like the cash for your honeymoon. A young bride-to-be recently asked me if that was possible, and I unfortunately had to tell her not to expect rolls of cash as gifts. She thought that if she didn't register anywhere, her guests would have no choice but to give her cash, checks, and stocks. That kind of logic—or lack of logic—doesn't work in this case.

The men and children are invited

Since this is not a traditional shower, the guest list is usually non-traditional as well. The men are usually invited, as couples' showers are more popular now. And why shouldn't the men join in the fun? Why shouldn't the groom get to open gifts and enjoy the attention as well?

If you have kids, they may host the shower. Some second-time brides and mothers have told me how adorable their kid-planned showers were, as the children were given a sizeable budget for the plans and they chose the menu, decorations, and favors. One woman told me of her daughter's beautifully arranged tea party, complete with Twinkies and Oreos. The guests loved it, and the daughter glowed with pride. Another couple told me of their teenage daughter's outdoor brunch with vegetable lasagna, quiche, and fruit salad. The daughter was a vegetarian, and she planned a lovely spread that—for once—she could fully partake of. Whatever the plans your kids make, it will be a special event because they did it for you.

Registries

Most brides register at more than one place these days, so you should feel free to register wherever you'd like. You can sign up for a new dish set at Fortunoff and a line of garden tools at Home Depot. Over the past few years, registry options have exploded in variety, and the many online options make registering easier for you and accessing your registry easier for your guests. Here, you'll consider more of your registry wishes, and you'll also learn how to avoid those garage-sale-bound gifts.

Registry possibilities

In the Resources section of this book, you will find a detailed list of registries available at some of the most popular national department and specialty stores. As you consider your registry options, you may use these, or you may seek out other stores in your area that offer registry service. For a detailed explanation of items available in various stores in every region of the United States, check out Leah Ingram's *Bridal Registry Book*.

Today's bride is registering for everything from china and crystal to skis and camping equipment. One bride I spoke to said she wanted wallpaper borders, paint, and stenciling supplies from Home Depot, which is fast becoming one of the most popular registry locations. At Pier 1 Imports, you can find dishes and a vast selection of glasses, candles, and even furniture and artwork for your home.

You might choose to start your own valuable wine collection with a registry at a winery or specialty liquor store. Some grooms are registering for cigar humidors and particular brands of cigars, and couples are recording their online wish lists at amazon.com for their book, software, and music wishes.

So consider your needs and goals, your shared interests, and the accessibility of your registry, and have fun filling out your own wish lists in several useful areas.

Registering well

How can you register well? It's something I've instructed brides to do after making my own registry mistakes and talking to other brides about theirs.

Registering well means really taking a look at what you need, and not registering for items that sound like fun but are not practical. Go through catalogs. See what's out there. See if your baking pans really do need to be upgraded, if you really need new silverware, or if you really need new china. Register only for what you will use on a regular basis.

Another aspect of registering well is making sure you are specific about what you want. Although most registries require that you put a model number for any item you choose, some brides skip this step, thinking that any model will do. But you might wind up with an inferior product. So use model numbers whenever possible. When registering for artwork, specify the artist. When registering for books, name the genre or author. For wines, name the vintage. It will do you no good to amass a collection of inferior bottles. Always be specific when it comes it any item name, color, size, or description.

Consider your guests' budgets when you register. Some of your guests may be able to shop in the $100 range, but others may only be able to afford a $30 present. Be sure your registry offers inexpensive items that your financially limited loved ones can choose as well.

Always put down "gift certificates welcome," as many people prefer to give a gift that allows you to get what you truly need. Some brides report that they preferred gift certificates and did not consider them tacky gifts at all. They received gift certificates for dinner at a favorite restaurant, which was a welcome outing after the return from the honeymoon. Others report that they loved having a stack of gift certificates for their favorite store, and that they could just indulge in a free shopping spree for whatever they desired. Offering this option lets some of your guests off the hook, and it's a great way to be sure you'll get the right items for your home or use.

Put your address on the registry as well, so that guests who will not be attending will feel free to send a gift to your home. Of course, you can't instruct them to do this, but putting your address on the registry facilitates their sending out of the goodness of their hearts. Some registries do offer free delivery to the bride's home, so check that option as well.

The key to registering well is to prioritize your needs. Think about what you and your partner can use to enjoy your time together, improve your home, or share with your kids. Then find the right, well-known registries, and sign up for your items. Inform your maids about where you're registering, and they will take the correct word-of-mouth course and notify your loved ones.

Part Three

Planning the Reception

Chapter 15

The Elements of Your Style

A rranging for all of the elements of your reception is a hectic, detail-filled task—which may strain you in your already hectic, detail-filled life—but it can also be one of the most enjoyable parts of the planning process. After all, you're creating the details of your celebration, giving your event a "look" and a "feel," and finally bringing into reality all of the special touches that you've wanted for your event.

This section will help you consider the basic elements of your reception, from menu selection, to cake tastings, to choosing memorable, unique favors that will impress. The style of your wedding, whether outdoor informal or indoor formal, will dictate some of your decisions and will guide you to a world of existing ideas in the industry. It will start your motor running and begin the flow of new ideas that you can use to bring more life and individuality to your wedding.

Most brides report having much more fun planning their receptions the second time around. Julie Weingarden, a recent second-time bride, says that her reception was finally *her* reception, not her mother's. Julie echoes a familiar sentiment among most brides, and all of the women I spoke to said that they were far more pleased with the reception they planned for their second weddings than those that were held for them during their first. The second time around, the parents may not be holding the purse strings and thus the decision-making power. Also, the couple themselves may have more money to spend on a celebration that is truly of their nature and style.

Couples who have kids say that they planned their receptions with their children in mind, remembering to add kid-friendly items to the menu in order to suit their children's picky palates. For these parents, theme weddings helped the children get excited about the wedding; many even asked the kids for their input on some of the decisions.

You have a great deal of freedom in planning your reception. At this time in our society, you do not have to adhere to old customs that restrict the size and scope of your celebration. The wedding industry knows that second-time weddings are a large chunk of its customer base, and it caters to you now to help you create the reception of your dreams.

So now, let's begin planning your reception.

How style and formality affect your decisions

You already know from earlier chapters how the style of your wedding will affect the details you plan. If you're having an outdoor garden wedding, your decor will match your surroundings and the style of your celebration. Your menu too, in this situation, will depend on your style and formality. You may choose passed hors d'oeuvres, a light luncheon buffet, or even buffet stations that meet all of your guests' needs.

Your caterer or planner can explain the possibilities of your area to you. If you live in New England and are having a beach wedding, you may choose a beach clambake with all the trimmings in keeping with that traditional New England style. If you live in New York City, you may choose to have an elegant ball in a museum or high-class hotel, and your menu will reflect those surroundings, by including such foods as pate, salmon provinciale, beluga caviar, and the like.

An entire book could be written on customizing your reception to the style and formality of your wedding, and when you add in the unlimited factors of personal style and expression, there is simply no way that I can provide you with all of the information you need. What I can do is start your reception planning process off by bringing your attention back to the style and formality of your wedding, reminding you that these rules do apply, and that you will most likely gravitate toward suitable ideas on your own or with the help of your caterer.

How caterers and planners can help

You may not be aware of all of the options that are open to you, as I certainly wasn't when I began to research this book. Your only experiences and frame of reference may come from what you see in magazines, what you've seen at other weddings and events, and what you see on television. But you have access to a great deal of new ideas that may ring true for you and may fit in perfectly with the wedding you wish to plan. That is the influence of a talented caterer, chef, or event planner.

These wedding professionals, if appropriately accredited and experienced, have an endless supply of wonderful, creative ideas for weddings of all types. Their personal talents have led them to their careers, and they earn their reputations through the events they have planned in the past. Good caterers, chefs, or planners can share with you the details or pictures of events they've planned in the past, and they can bring up new ideas that may delight you.

Diane Forden, editor-in-chief of *Bridal Guide*, speaks highly of the existing trend in reception planning through well-trained and experienced caterers and chefs. "Caterers today are not looking to plan the same wedding over and over," she says. "They understand that their clientele is diverse and that the couples and guests are *far* more sophisticated than those of years past. They have to appeal to many different taste levels, and they are willing to work with you to create the perfect reception menu for our style."

The days of chicken and beef entrees and the predictable buffet options are over. Now, chefs and caterers know that their clients—that's you—have broad tastes for exotic foods and elegant meal presentations and preparations. The standard chicken dish, the reliable standby for more inexpensive menu options, appears now in enough different forms to fill a cookbook. Chefs know how to prepare basic foods in a myriad of ways, and they are knowledgeable of menu combinations that will suit your requests.

You may be surprised after meeting with your menu facilitator, whether it be a chef, caterer, or planner, at how open your choices are, at the extent of the menu possibilities, and at all of the other issues that arise. For instance, event planner Shirley Feuerstein of Affairs and Arrangements in New Jersey says that couples and their guests are far more informed about wines now. They make their selections regarding the menu with some thought to the types of wines and liquors they will be serving at the reception. Guests are savvier about food. They have tastes for the exotic, for

Indian food and Thai cuisine, for a variety of beef and chicken dishes. They lean away from pasta options and choose instead menu items that are not the usual wedding fare. A good caterer or chef will know this and will suggest it to you, but—and this is important—he will not be so excited about creating an international taste-off that he does not remember to include some standard dishes that children and less adventurous guests will like. Not everyone has a taste for curry, and you do not want your guests to complain that there is nothing that they like on the menu. So although your ability to create a stellar menu is there, remember to include some more traditional options for your guests' sake.

As always, interview caterers and chefs thoroughly, make appointments to review their catering menus, and always plan for a tasting. A good chef will allow you to come in and taste his creations, so that you know the quality of the food that will be offered at your wedding. Guests remember three things about weddings: how you look, the entertainment, and the food. But it is the food they most often discuss in the car on the way home.

A talk with an award-winning chef

I spoke to Jerome Louie, head chef of the Bernards Inn in Bernardsville, New Jersey, about his experiences with second-time weddings. His wonderfully candid advice guides you here with regard to originality, money-saving ideas, and the benefits of a top-notch chef or caterer when planning any wedding. As you might expect, he asks that the couple come in and discuss their wedding style, formality, size, and budget, and he guides them through their possibilities. Advice from Jerome Louie:

- Consider the time of day of your wedding. An afternoon wedding usually means a lighter menu with less expensive food options.
- An afternoon wedding or a Sunday wedding usually means that your guests will drink less liquor than they would for a Friday night or Saturday night wedding. Know that the time of day you've chosen will affect your open or consumption bar policies and expenses.
- As a chef, I can be extremely creative with any menu option you suggest. If you want a chicken entrée, I can be quite flexible and creative about all of the different kinds of chicken dishes that can be available for you. While you may want chicken because it is less expensive than beef, I can still create a unique chicken dish that will impress your guests, add variety to your menu, and not cost you a fortune.

◈ Check your contract carefully for the pricing of entrée options. Some caterers charge differently for the types of foods you select, or for the aspect of having two different entrée options to choose from. It may not always be standard. It may be an extra expense.

◈ A good chef and banquet hall like ours will work with you to create a personalized menu. While we do offer a standard package with a pre-scribed menu for couples who just want to accept our high-quality pre-selected choices, we are completely open to mix-and-matching and adding new options to your list.

The liquor question

Your guests will probably be quite savvy about wines and spirits. Again, you're in luck, as the wedding industry now accepts that fine vintages of wine and champagne and top-shelf liquors and liqueurs are given high priority in the planning of a wedding. No longer will your guests find as their only options "house whites" or "house reds." Your liquor selections will be every bit as important as your food selections, and you should either learn about wines or depend upon a knowledgeable friend to select the vintages that are right for your wedding.

As you know, certain types of wines go with certain types of foods; red with beef, white with fish, and so on. But the rules and intricacies of the wine and liquor world run far deeper now that the general public has taken a greater interest in winemaking and the selection of the right bottles.

Many second-time couples familiarize themselves with the rules of the wine world by taking wine-tasting classes, where they learn the differences between types of wines and the suitability of each type. If you do not have the time or money for wine-tasting classes, you might choose to spend several months ordering something other than your usual brand of wine when you go out to dinner. Try out Kendall Jackson, Chateau St. Jean, and various merlots. Learn which types you like.

If you need further guidance, consult with the experts at *www.winespectator.com*, the Web site of the prestigious wine information magazine, where you will find ratings of the best, award-winning vintages, descriptions and reviews of taste, and detailed lists of which kinds of wines go with precise types of menus. This Web site is invaluable if you plan to give attention to your wine and champagne at the wedding, and you may begin a lifelong love of wine knowledge and a shared interest with your husband-to-be.

As far as hard liquor, most brides report that their guests prefer the top-shelf brands. Again, your guests may be older and more sophisticated than they were at your first wedding. They have certainly had more exposure to the finer things in life since the days of college when they drank cheap beer or wine coolers. Now, they want their Grand Marnier or their Louis XIV. They enjoy their Grey Goose, and they know the difference between Cristal and other champagnes. Provide them with the best, even if you have to limit the categories of liquors offered in order to protect your budget.

Drinking is not so much the emphasis of the second-time wedding. Although many first-time brides marry in their early to mid-20s, and their guests are their high school and college friends who still have that college propensity for shots and beer, your guests are likely to control themselves enough so as not to turn your wedding into a frat-house bash. At most second-time weddings you are more likely to find guests holding themselves to a responsible drinking limit, strolling around with glasses of champagne or fine Chardonnay. There may be some glassy eyes and some extra-loud laughter at the end of the night (it may even be yours) but by far, alcohol is not greatly emphasized at second weddings.

It is almost unheard of for second-time weddings to have a cash bar (as it is for most weddings in general). So please adjust your beverage offerings to what you can afford per guest. I do not encourage cash bars, as your guests should not have to pay for their own drinks throughout the day and night.

Cakes

The wedding cake is an art form in itself. Just a decade ago, the industry varied very slightly from the usual white cake with strawberry filling and straight icing with scalloped edges. Add the plastic bride and groom on top, and you have the image of the wedding cake that's been the standard for decades upon decades.

Now, wedding cakes are sculptures. They are crafted by experts whose talents surpass those of painters. The very famous Sylvia Weinstock, cake creator to the stars, and her staff of artists shared with me the cake trends they are seeing for all types of weddings, whether first or second, formal or informal.

The first step: your cake needs

You're unlikely to go without a wedding cake, although I have seen some glorious arrangements of pastries and beautifully frosted cupcakes arranged in tiers to resemble a wedding cake. For the regular cake of many layers, you will need to shop well for a quality baker, do taste tests, and think again about the style, formality, and size of your wedding.

At your meeting with the baker you have chosen, supply her with the following information:

1. **The date and time of your wedding.** This is necessary for her scheduling, so that you allow her to book her valuable time for the creation of your cake. The best bakers only take on so many jobs per weekend so that they can devote themselves to the artistry needed for cake design.
2. **Whether or not your wedding will be held outdoors.** The baker needs to know what kinds of conditions her cake will face. For outdoor weddings in the summertime, the icing will need to be buttercream, which can stand up to hot weather. Bakers know about cakes that melt due to exposure to the elements, and they want to match up their supplies with the needs of your day.
3. **What the style or theme of your wedding is.** A truly creative baker can match the icing design to the lace or details of your gown. If you have planned a beach wedding, your designer may be able to decorate your cake with delicate seashells or starfish made of gumpaste.
4. **What your tastes are as far as appearance of the cake.** Some brides love the tall, tiered look, others want offset tiers, others don't want tiers at all. The best way to handle this is to bring in pictures of cakes that appeal to you, and let the designer work from that.

The design of cakes

The second-time bride takes a lot of freedom with the design of her cake. She does not feel bound to have the traditional, three-tiered cake with white icing and columns between each layer. Now, you can choose from different shapes and arrangements, from round cakes to square cakes, from tiers to single-layer cakes, and even cupcakes or petit fours for the most informal, outdoor party.

Frosting is no longer just evenly spread white frosting with the piped-on scallop edging and rosettes. Rolled fondant, the flat, matte icing featured on Martha Stewart's magazine covers for years, is still a most popular variation on the buttercream look (you've seen the wedding cakes that look like wrapped gifts, complete with gumpaste ribbons) the decor of cakes now runs the gamut in design. You will see straight icing with pearl designs of colored icing drops. The fondant comes into play with a basket-weave design. Icings can be tinted to match your color scheme, although this option is advisable only for the most pale pastel colors. No one wants a bright blue or orange cake, even if it goes with the theme.

Those plastic bride and groom cake toppers are a thing of the past, as well. You may not even see them stocked in bakeries anymore. Now, the look is a cascade of fresh flowers, either all in one color or in a vibrant selection of colors and shapes. Your florist can help you select the right flowers for your cake decor, and she can be hired to do the arrangement of those flowers on the cake immediately before the wedding. It is most important that the flowers be applied fresh and clean to your cake, so that they make the greatest appearance.

Other dessert options

Most weddings now offer more than just the wedding cake as a dessert option for guests. The Viennese table set-up allows your guests to choose from cheesecakes, mousses, pastries, bananas foster, flambees, fruit trays with fresh whipped cream, and fruit tarts with chantilly cream.

Because your wedding may not be the traditional type, you might incorporate some other dessert options. For more informal weddings, perhaps you will provide chocolate mousse cakes or pies or a big fresh fruit salad.

Second-time brides with children and lots of child guests at the wedding often set up an ice cream sundae bar for the kids to create their own desserts. Often, even the adults partake of this offering, building their own banana splits. Guests usually rave about the considerate and original inclusion of such an option.

Groom's cake

The option of a separate groom's cake is not just for the southern wedding anymore. Gail Watson of Gail Watson Cake Designs still maintains the old tradition of boxing a small piece of fruitcake to give to the single women at the wedding. The women are supposed to place the box under their pillows at night, and tradition has it that they will then dream of the men they will someday marry. Although not too many people espouse that practice, the groom's cake still showcases at weddings in the form of petit fours, boxed and wrapped or beribboned attractively. To view Gail Watson's designs and prices, check out her Web site at *www.gailwatsoncake.com.* There, you will also find pictures and descriptions of lovely sugar flower napkin rings, sugar gift boxes for favors, wedding cake cookies, and the traditional wedding favor—Jordan almonds wrapped in tulle or placed in boxes.

Speaking of favors

Lovely memories are not the only thing your guests will bring home with them of your perfect day; they will also bring home your choice of favors as a memento of your wedding. Although the aforementioned sugared almonds are still a popular choice for favors—symbolic as they are of the sweetness of marriage—wedding favors vary tremendously. Several years ago, personalized wine bottles were very popular.

Today, favors reflect the style of the celebration. Outdoor, garden weddings see small plants or fall bulbs as favors. Formal weddings see crystal heart vases and silver frames. The variations on favors vary as much as the fingerprints of the bride and groom. Some are more posh, purchased from designer Web sites, and others are more personal and homemade. Consider your wedding style and what you would like your guests to take home as a lasting memory of your day. Know that it's best to give your guests something they can use or display rather than something they can eat or quickly use up. Here are some popular options:

- Silver frames with photos.
- Glass bowls with silver tops, filled with potpourri or good luck river stones.
- Plants, flowers, seedlings, bulbs, and flower seeds with instructions.
- Candleholders and scented candles.
- Crystal vases or candy dishes.
- Gift certificates for spa services.
- Small bottles of champagne.
- Clocks.
- Silver key chains.

A very popular choice right now is music CDs, on which the guests will find a selection of "your" songs or notable songs from the wedding day. Companies such as *www.cdnow.com* will offer you a list of the songs they supply, and you customize your mixes for beautifully-designed CDs your guests will enjoy. Mix well, though. The best CD favors are collections of love songs, romantic music to make love to, jazz classics, or celebration songs.

Some brides warn against getting personalized bottles of wine or other liquors as favors, as they may have some recovering alcoholics or diabetics in their midst.

Plant bulbs are also highly popular, as you are giving your guests a symbol of new life, of growth, of new beginnings. You'll find special wedding favor bulbs packaged in specially designed boxes with card quotes, or personalized packets of flower seeds, at Tree and Floral Beginnings, *www.plantamemory.com*. The popular Forever and Always company offers labeled packets of violet, daisy, forget-me-not, lunaria, carnation, and other seeds on their Web site *www.foreverandalways.com*. You may be able to spend less by buying your favorite type of regionally appropriate bulbs at your local garden store and boxing or wrapping them in tulle for a pretty presentation.

For a while, socially or environmentally conscious couples chose to have donations to charity serve as their guests' "favors." These donations obviously have their merits, but they often garner mixed reactions from guests. Several brides reported that their guests were offended by receiving a card that read, "In thanks for your attendance at our wedding, we have donated $50 to the _____ organization in your name." Wedding author Leah Ingram has heard the backlash too, as she shared with me the reviews of other wedding couples she spoke to: "People don't know how to react to that kind of favor," Ingram says. "Some ask if that makes their favor a tax write-off for the wedding couple."

Aside from the potential tax questions, some guests dislike the fact that money was donated in their name to a charity that they may not believe in. Although it may not be the case that the guest does not believe in the fundamental cause of a certain environmental association, the problem may be that the guest knows that particular cause supports a political party that they dislike. Or, they may know that the charity you've chosen gives only a small percentage of its received funds into the actual support work it is supposed to be doing. So although giving to charity is an honorable practice, it might best be left out of your wedding favor ideas.

The most popular wedding favor today is the Godiva chocolate box, the gold-foiled gift that is as recognizable for its wrapping as Tiffany's blue box. Nothing in the industry says elegance—at such a surprisingly low cost—as well as a Godiva gift box of two or four pieces of chocolate. For a small extra charge, your local Godiva store can accent the gift box with any color ribbon, imprinted or not, for an extra special effect.

Chapter 16

Entertainment

Besides the food and how you look in your gown, the entertainment is what sticks in your guests' memories. Your wedding is a celebration, and the entertainment you provide sets the tone and the mood for the entire event. A great musician or DJ who knows how to read and lead his audience can turn your reception into an unforgettable evening that is at turns outrageously fun, touching, tender, and romantic.

Music has been a large part of the tradition of weddings, from the days of the pan flute processions of the Dark Ages to the drumbeats of the African plains, to the delicate harp songs at a royal wedding. Luckily, the trends in wedding music have gone way beyond the usual five-piece band or the DJ in the sequined jacket. Now, you can have a unique blend of entertainment at your custom-designed wedding, as the music at your reception will express who you are and your commitment to each other. Please note that you do not have to choose only one type of entertainer. Many brides choose several—a harpist for the cocktail hour, a DJ for the reception, and a jazz pianist to close out the evening.

Here, you'll think about the entertainment for your wedding, as the vision you have begins to take on some sound and some dimension. You'll learn to choose the right entertainer for your style of celebration, how to keep the kids entertained, and how to *be* the entertainment for your own turns in the spotlight.

What fits your style?

The entertainment will, of course, have to fit the style of the wedding; classical music for an ultra-formal wedding or more current hits for a semi-formal one. But as important as it is for the music to match the events and style of your reception, it's even more important that the entertainment match your personal style. Your guests will be perplexed if you have an all-harp musical ensemble at your reception when you're a more hip person with a wide range of musical tastes.

The best way to assess the entertainment according to your style is to map out the events of the reception and imagine what kinds of music you want offered at each "station." The usual reception offers classical music or easy-listening, piano, or harp during the cocktail hour, a progression from slow songs to faster songs during the dancing part of the evening, and party songs at the end of the evening. Think about the acts of your reception and see what would be appropriate for your cocktail hour, the progression of your reception, and the after-hours time.

What suits your guests' styles

The previous section asked you to search your own style to create the entertainment picture for your wedding. Recent brides suggest that you avoid the temptation to use all one kind of music, thinking that an entire evening of love songs is going to please your guests. It may seem romantic to you to have an endless string of slow dances for your mostly married guests to sway to, but you should venture out of the usual to provide a variety of music for everyone.

Remember that you'll have guests of varying ages and backgrounds who would like to dance to music they love, so search your own style for which kinds of songs in various genres touch a chord with you. Here are some examples:

- Current hits that teenagers can dance to.
- Always popular: 1980s music that everyone knows.
- Songs from the 1940's that your older guests can dance to. Younger guests will love watching Grandma twirling on the dance floor with Grandpa, or the pairs doing the Peabody or the Lindy.

You don't have to play kid's music, as the children will adapt well to any type of music. At a recent second wedding I attended, I was amazed to see a little blond 8-year-old flower girl dancing to Frank Sinatra tunes. The older teenagers will be a little bit harder to please, but they should be taken into account to some degree when planning a reception. If your children are of that age, ask them to submit a short list of the songs they want to hear at the wedding. You approve and then hand the list to the DJ or band. This step has proven to be a successful one for new, blending families, as the kids appreciate having a voice in that decision, in having their preferences noted, and in having the promise of at least a few songs they can dance to. It may even be a bonding experience when you dance with them to their favorite songs. You may not know the words, but you'll get credit from the kids for even being out on the dance floor.

Always make sure your entertainment is varied. Even for a beach or outdoor wedding, mix up the wedding music with the celebration music, as that is the trend in entertainment for second-time weddings.

Entertainment for the kids

If your guest list includes a lot of children, perhaps including your own, you may want to arrange for some kind of entertainment for them. Some brides who plan outdoor weddings with a tent set up a separate play area for the kids and hire a babysitter to run activities for them. Or, you might choose to hire a children's entertainer such as a character in a costume to make a special appearance and hand out games and kid-friendly snacks.

Children do get bored, tired, and cranky during the long day and night of a wedding, so it is important to have an agenda for them. Do not expect them to sit like little ladies and gentlemen during the formal events of the reception, as you are inviting attention-getting tantrums and wild runarounds. Provide them with something to do so that the wedding is fun for them, and so that their parents can have a few turns on the dance floor.

Ethnic inclusions

Consider incorporating some of your ethnic backgrounds into the reception. You may not choose an all-Irish theme or an all-Italian theme, but you might select a few specialty dances or traditions for a long and fruitful life together. For instance, at a Ukrainian wedding I recently attended, the bride and groom (a second wedding for her and a first for him) were met at the entrance to the reception by their parents, who offered them a tray of bread ("may you always have food on your table"), salt ("there will always be some bitterness in life"), and wine ("but there will also be sweetness.") The couple ate the salted bread, then drank of the wine, honoring an old and beautiful tradition from their heritage.

Do some research on your heritage's wedding customs. Many Web sites exist for all nationalities, and the wedding Web sites do have some limited suggestions for traditions you might like to include. Or, you might follow the trend in which professional dancers from an ethnic dance troupe come in to perform a few numbers for the crowd. As one professional ethnic dancer told me, "The guests love it. They come to a wedding, having traveled perhaps a long distance, they've given an expensive gift, and they're happy to see a show in return. They love the unique aspect of it as well."

Including ethnic traditions also teaches your children more about their own background and those that their blended family's interaction will now bring into their lives.

Hiring musicians and entertainers

The selection process of your entertainer is an important job. If you want quality entertainment that will enhance your wedding and not detract from it, you will need to search and audition well in order to find the right entertainer who will fit your style of wedding.

Of course, you should begin by getting referrals from family and friends. Who played their wedding or corporate event? Were they a smash? Ask about the inside information, as some entertainers who put on a great show at the event you attended may actually have been difficult to work with behind the scenes. Ask your contacts what it was really like to work with their chosen entertainers.

Don't immediately go with the band or DJ that has the biggest and most impressive ad in the phone book. That might simply mean that they charge a lot and have a good pool of advertising money. Just include the names that catch your eye in your search list.

You can save a lot of time by calling around *on weekdays* to see if the band or DJ is even available on the day of your wedding. It will do no good to get into particulars if they're not even in the running, so a simple "Do you have any openings on May 25th?" will do.

One of the most important aspects of this stage, and one that can save you a lot of time and frustration, is the full disclosure of the details of your wedding. Your entertainers will need to know which locations you are considering, what power sources will be available at outdoor wedding sites, and whether or not they will be sheltered from possible wind or rain. They'll need to know about platforms on which they'll perform, the sizes of the rooms, the numbers of guests, and—perhaps most importantly—your budget.

When you interview, be sure the entertainer has the kinds of music you thought about earlier. Ask for a selection, and be sure there is a wide enough range of songs to please your guests. Entertainers should be able to fax a complete list of their available songs and offer to get any specific songs you need.

Although viewing a standard videotape of them in action may seem like a good idea—and they may push their carefully edited tapes on you—always interview and audition the bands and DJs first. Ask if you can see them in action at another event, if possible.

At each potential entertainer's interview and audition, find out the following:

- How many weddings they've done.
- How willing they are to accommodate your requests.
- Whether their style suits the style of your wedding (are they too energetic, too over-the-top, too laid back?).
- What they will be wearing. (Can you request that they wear a certain color beyond the basic black suit?)

Watch them set up their equipment, see how they interact with each other, and ask them to perform a slow song, a party song, and "your" song. Some bands have the three songs they play at every audition, and they're pretty much only good at those songs. This is an audition and an interview, so see what their range is.

Submitting your song list

When you submit your requested song list to the entertainer, remember that this list is flexible. Your DJ or band will be sure to provide these songs for you, but they will be open to other requests from your guests. Most entertainers provide this service, and they do stick to your wishes.

Start your list by recording which songs you want played for the traditional dances:

- Your first dance as bride and groom.
- Your dances with your parents (optional).
- A song for the bridal party.
- A song for your children.
- The songs you want played during the cutting of the cake, the tossing of the bouquet and the garter, and any other wedding standards you choose to implement on your day.
- A song for the longest-married couple in the room.

Once the specifics are down, choose your song list according to type of music. Your list might look like this:

Songs for the reception hour:
- "Winter" by George Winston.
- "Four Seasons" by Antonio Vivaldi.
- "Barcelona" by Andrea Boccelli and Sarah Brightman.

General party songs:
- "Ain't Too Proud to Beg," by The Temptations.
- "Brown Eyed Girl," by Van Morrison.
- "Build Me Up Buttercup," by The Foundations.
- "Conga," by Miami Sound Machine.
- "Devil With the Blue Dress," by Mitch Ryder (perfect if your maids are in blue).
- "Mack the Knife," by Bobby Darin.
- "Stand By Me," by Ben E. King/John Lennon.
- "Unforgettable," by Nat King Cole and Natalie Cole.
- "What I Like About You," by The Romantics.

What don't you want?

Besides submitting a list of songs that you want to hear at your wedding, you should also take control of the entertainment portion of your reception by mandating what you *don't* want to hear. This list might include wedding songs from your first marriages, a song that reminds you of someone else, a song that has a derogatory message, or a song that hits a harsh nerve with some of your guests. You should speak with your entertainer about the specific songs he is not to play at your wedding. You don't have to explain why. Just submit the list. Ask your groom to do the same, as he may have associations to songs as well; most of us do.

Many second-time brides also put on their do-not-subject-me-to-this list the songs that are played at every wedding, such as the Chicken Dance, the Macarena, the Electric Slide, or any other line dance they might have an aversion to. Those songs are played at so many weddings that your guests may be thankful for their exclusion at yours.

Other commonly excluded entertainment options:

- Father-daughter dance.
- Mother-son dance.
- Bouquet toss.
- Garter toss.
- Dollar dance.
- Some ethnic or religious elements that others want, but you don't.

Mixing your own music

You might choose to create your own music soundtracks for your wedding. Especially at informal home weddings, brides and grooms often provide their own music by recording the songs that they like best. Some spend the time to create varied mixes, and others load their six favorite CDs into their machine for continuous playing of the music they love. This is a popular option, as it means no one has to man the CD player all night. So if your wedding style allows for this more informal musical source, use a multi-CD player.

Dazzle them with your dancing

You can *be* the entertainment by showing off your dancing skills to your guests. Too many brides and grooms perform their first dance just swaying back and forth, maybe moving in a slow circle, and the guests watch for a minute or two. They've seen it all before. But at your wedding, you can give them something to really watch. Join the trend among wedding couples by taking dance lessons a few months before your wedding. That way, your first dance will be an impressive spin around the floor, with lots of perfectly executed footwork, turns, and dips. Throughout the rest of the night, you can steal the spotlight again with your tango, cha-cha, and salsa dancing.

Most brides report that their grooms were initially reluctant to go to dance lessons, but that they learned the steps rather easily and enjoyed the boost in confidence. At the wedding, they were far more likely to dance, they were more loose and relaxed, and they danced with more guests. The brides themselves said they shared the same benefits, and the lessons would give them a shared activity that they could enjoy as a couple in the future. It's a win-win situation, one that comes highly recommended by a vast number of brides and grooms.

Chapter 17

Photography and Videography

Of course, you'll want to capture the images of your wedding day on film so that you can go back and revisit your wedding day for as long as you both shall live. The wedding photography and videography world has changed in recent years, as upgraded technology means that higher quality images can be captured and printed. Photography style has changed from stiff poses in front of a standard background to more casual shots with prettier, more natural backgrounds. Wedding photo and video professionals are calling themselves "wedding photojournalists" and "wedding video journalists," giving the message that they are capturing special moments and documenting the day.

As you'll see in photographers' and videographers' samples, the pictures are more vibrant, more energetic, and more like the photo spreads you see in magazines. The posed shots are mostly gone and candids are in. Black and white footage, either in portraits or in sections of video, are more popular as well for those who decorate their homes in modern black and white tones.

Although the trends dictate what you'll see on the market, you are always free to request the style and tone of the images you want for your personal displays and gifts to others. In this section, you'll arrange for your photographer and videographer, choosing the best professional and package for you.

Wedding photography

Although you may already know the basics—such as interviewing highly regarded professionals and viewing their sample books—from planning your first wedding, this time around you may need to make decisions that are more suited to who you are right now. Perhaps your parents had a lot of input as to the photos you chose for your package the first time around. Coming from their background of stiff, posed shots, they may not have had a lot of knowledge about the newer styles of photos.

Now you know the types of photos you want. You know if you want traditional, posed group shots, action shots, or "stolen moments" shots. You know if you want the romantic look created with a gauzy lens, or a sleek black and white look. At the outset, discuss your personal style with the photographer and be sure he or she can provide you with what you want.

Hiring tips for photographers

Take some advice from many brides with these extra tips about hiring photographers:

- Be sure they've done your kind of wedding before. If your wedding will be held outdoors, make sure they've done outdoor weddings in the past and know how to adapt to the changing light circumstances.
- Be sure they can work your site. Some photographers will not do beach weddings because of potential damage to their equipment.
- Discuss what they will wear. If you're not having a formal wedding, where a standard tuxedo would be worn, talk to the professional about your wishes for his wardrobe.
- Ask about the photographer's transportation needs. Inform them of any travel needs for the wedding day, such as ceremony and reception sites at long, difficult distances from each other.
- Be sure to get a cell phone number for contact on the wedding day.
- It's a plus if they are members of a professional organization, such as Wedding Portrait Photographers International or Professional Photographers of America. These organizations inform their members about new technology in the field, new editing options, and better materials. If they're better informed, they can offer you a better product.

- ❧ Specify the times you'll need them, and when and where they should show up on the morning of the wedding.
- ❧ Find out how long it will take to get your proofs and albums back. A good photographer has a fast turnaround time, depending upon the type of film you've used.
- ❧ Be sure they're open to your personalized instructions and are not so set in their ways as to be inflexible for you.
- ❧ **Very important:** Specify the amount of time they get to take the post-ceremony pictures. You don't want to miss half of your reception because you're taking an endless lineup of shots.

Assembling a package you will actually use

Your photographer will have a standard list of the shots he typically takes for wedding packages. Feel free to choose from that list and add ideas of your own. Because your wedding is an individual entity, and your family situation is also equally unique, I'll leave it up to you to create your list of needed shots.

Again, you know what you want to display in your home. You also know what your family members will want to display. Cindi Dixon of Silver Studios in Lancaster, Pennsylvania spoke of a bride's mother who wanted a portrait of her daughter that would be similar in style to the portrait she already had of her other daughter. The bride didn't want any old-fashioned shots, but she worked with the photographer to take a shot for her mother, and then return to the style she had chosen. You too may need to ask for certain shots to appease family members, but you should always put your wishes first for this task. These are your pictures, and the choices are up to you.

Videography

Luckily, the advent of the newer, smaller, digital video cameras means you won't have the interruption of a videographer hefting a huge piece of machinery on his shoulder. The smaller models of cameras available today allow the video professional to blend more into the crowd and not make such a scene while capturing images.

Again, you know to interview your video professionals, see their finished work, check out the packages offered by size and price, and inform them of all specifics about the style, size, and locations of the wedding.

What you may not know at this point is that you have several options for wedding videography packages. You can ask for the videographers to use a high quality digital camera, which will give a high quality image even on such less expensive film stocks as Hi-8 and VHS. A good camera will produce great images, and you need not spend even more for the best in film stock. This may be the only wedding area where it's safe to choose a less expensive option.

What kind of editing do you want?

You're paying for the editing time as well as the time it takes the videographer to shoot the details of your day. Videographer Steve Blahitka of Back East Productions in East Hanover, New Jersey says that you'll pay top dollar if you choose a highly-edited package, the top of the line with all special effects and editing abilities. Very often, it's the videos with a minimum of special effects and editing that turn out the best. Some couples ask for too many effects, and the editing overshadows their true images. To remain the stars of your own video, limit the effects you ask for.

Blahitka also offers a popular and inexpensive option with the selection of an unedited videotape. "I shoot the wedding with one camera in real time, choosing the elements to get with the right lighting and sound, and then at the end of the night I hand over the tape to the bride and groom. They don't have to wait, and they don't have to pay as much as if I spent 10 hours editing the tape down to an hour." Many couples choose this option to save themselves some money, as videotape packages can be very expensive. Most videographers do have experience with this kind of taping, and although you won't get the advantage of three camera angles and more seamless editing, you will still get great coverage of your event.

A conversation with your videographer

As with your photographer, you will want to make sure your video professional has reliable transportation and a cell phone, that he's planning on dressing appropriately, and that he has a list of what kinds of shots you want and don't want. What you do want to talk to the videographer about is interference. Videographers don't have the advantage of flashes for their required lighting, and some need to rely on big spotlights to adequately capture your event on film. Discuss the lighting situation of the sites where your ceremony and reception will take place, whether or not he'll deal with changing light elements, and what kind of lighting he provides.

Some videographers bring in big floodlights to light up the room, and the resulting footage is of all the dancing guests squinting and shielding themselves from the blinding, hot, white lights that have been installed throughout the room. Ask the videographer how often those lights will need to be turned on, or if there are any other lighting options you can discuss. A floodlight does not enhance a wedding ambiance, so see if you can limit the use of it or arrange for some other lighting.

Also important is sound. Discuss with your videographer the sound requirements for your wedding. If your wedding will be held outdoors, in a breezy meadow, or at the beach, the sound picked up by the camera and its microphones may be drowned out by the wind. Talk to your videographer about nature's influence on the sound you'll get for the video. He may have experience with beach weddings, and he may know how to microphone the two of you for better sound reception.

In addition, you'll have to let the videographer know about the interpersonal situation within your families. Let him know what footage you'd like to get, and what kind of diplomacy may be needed to get it. Submit a footage wish list, and specify what you don't want.

Remember, these are video journalists documenting your day, and as they say, "the camera sees all." When you return from your honeymoon and are able to view the completed tape, you might be surprised at what kinds of moments have been captured on film. You might get a view you didn't have on the day of your wedding of your groom gazing adoringly at you from across the room. You might get some footage of your kids finally warming up to their new stepsisters. And you may get a look at which kid stuck his fingers in the cake.

Chapter 18

Transportation

The most important thing on your wedding day may be taking your vows, but in order to do that, you've got to actually get there! You don't get to slip on the ring, taste those fabulous hors d'oeuvres, and smash cake in each other's faces if you're stuck on the side of a highway.

You shopped carefully for your florist and caterer, so you should do the same for your transportation company. Take some time, do some research, get referrals, and hire only the best. It goes without saying that all transportation companies should be searched through the Better Business Bureau and through the National Limousine Association (*www.nla.com*), but your best bet is to visit several companies and do your own personal research.

What's this going to cost?

Most limousines and classic cars are rented out for three-hour time slots. That is the basic wedding package for most companies, although you can arrange to rent a car for more or less time. The price, of course, is going to depend upon how many cars you need for all of your transportation requirements throughout the day. Remember that the men will need a ride to the ceremony site, you and your bridal party will need to get there, and everyone will need to get to and from the reception. Don't just count up your bridal party members and create your limo order based on that. Limousine companies rent 6-, 8-, 10-, and 12-seaters now, plus a variety of even bigger stretch vehicles, so you may be able to rent fewer cars. Speak with your rental agent about how many people you'll need to transport and where you'll be going. Most limousine companies do charge extra if they're expected to drive long distances, so keep that in mind.

Robert Bannon of America's Best Limousines in Fairfield, New Jersey offers smart limo shopping advice: "Always go with a company that prints its prices. We publish our price list and stick by it." That's one way to tell when a company has a code of ethics, which is important when you'll be depending on it for so much.

What kinds of cars are available?

Although the white stretch limousine is still the overwhelming favorite of most brides and grooms, other types of cars are available if you're the type who likes to make a unique statement or a grand entrance. For this wedding, you might prefer to arrive in any of the following:

- Rolls Royce.
- Bentley.
- Excalibur.

Very popular now are the unique and eye-catching array of stretch vehicles of all makes:

- Ford Expedition 4x4 24-passenger.
- Lexus GX 400 10-passenger.
- Mercedes Benz E420.
- BMW 750IL 10-passenger.
- Red Corvette 10-passenger.

These are just some of the newest trends in the industry right now, and you are free to ask your limousine companies about the variety of cars they offer.

One important thing to keep in mind when choosing which kind of car to go with is that limousines are, by law, the only kind of car in which you can drink champagne or other liquors. So if you'll plan on a private toast on the way to the reception, choose the limo.

You're not just limited to the white limousine, either. Silver and black are highly popular for weddings, and they are even slightly less expensive. If you choose a classic car or convertible for a less formal occasion, consider the colors open to you. White is fine for the bridal look, but some brides like to make their entrances in a brightly hued car. With all of the color options out there, the new vibrants, and even the pastels, you might even be able to match your car to the color scheme of your wedding.

Another option is the horse-drawn carriage. Although this is a romantic option, and it's certainly attention-getting and great for pictures, you must consider the logistics of such a decision. If it rains on your wedding day, you'll be exposed to the elements. A long traveling distance may be a nuisance with traffic, and it is a lot to ask of the horse and driver. Most horse and carriage companies have a distance and location limit, so their horses are not navigating super highways and difficult city roads.

Limousine shopping tips

It is important to check out the condition of the company's fleet of cars. Are they all relatively new? Are they clean? Are they in good repair? "Don't take a company's word that their cars will be fixed up a year from now," says Bannon. "If they're not in good shape now, move on to another company." A reputable company will let you not only see the cars from the outside but get inside them. Climb in, see if the car is spacious enough to accommodate either several people or that big, poofy gown you'll be wearing. Check for cleanliness, good condition of the seats, and (if this is important to you) whether or not the car smells of cigarette or cigar smoke. You can request a non-smoking car to be sure the ride will be a pleasant one on your wedding day.

Find out what else is included. Many transportation companies will throw in—for free—a red carpet leading up to the car door for your entrance as husband and wife. You may also get complimentary champagne set up in a champagne stand for an impromptu toast when the ceremony is over. Soda, bottled spring water, ice, and snacks are usually a part of the deal.

We've all heard stories about limos that break down, so be sure to address this with your vendor. A good company will have backup cars at the ready. America's Best Limos and other companies go an extra step: "We make sure our drivers have cell phones and two-way radios for constant, clear contact with home base. Cell phones don't work everywhere," says Bannon.

Ask what the drivers will be wearing, making sure that their wardrobe complements yours for the day. It is standard for most drivers to wear tuxedoes, and female drivers usually wear a similar tuxedo ensemble with black tie as well. Check with the manager to confirm your driver's appearance. While you're on the subject, find out how long your driver has been working with the company and how many weddings he has done. Ask for the company's best employee, as you deserve nothing but the best.

Provide a detailed instructions list to the company, complete with pickup and drop-off information, addresses, and phone numbers at those addresses. With this complete list of information, you have enabled the driver to call if he gets lost, and you've erased a potential wedding-day catastrophe.

Transportation for others

Many companies have party buses that can take your bridal party or your visiting guests from the hotel to the ceremony to the reception and back. Determine the size you'll need and ask for rates and times. Most brides report that their guests had such a great time on the party bus that they wish they'd been on board too. Right now, the wedding industry is seeing a big increase in demand for mini-buses for larger bridal parties. It is actually cheaper than renting five limos, and it enhances the party atmosphere.

Your hotel manager can also help out with transporting your guests to and from the wedding by offering the services of the hotel's shuttle bus. Very often, this is a free service if you've booked several rooms at the hotel or if you will be holding your reception in one of the hotel's banquet halls. Your guests will appreciate your taking the driving burden off of them, and it is a great way for you to ensure that none of your guests will drive drunk.

Of course, good-hearted friends, relatives, and bridal party members can volunteer to pick up and drop off guests either at the airport or the hotel, further facilitating your guests' needs. Schedule this way in advance so that your kind volunteer can manage the driving duties.

If you do your choosing wisely—as you did with your partner—you'll be secure in knowing that you won't have to worry about transportation on your wedding day. You'll arrive in style, you'll depart with class, and you'll share a kiss in the back of the car that will carry you off to your future—or at least to the part where you get to smash the cake in each other's faces.

Chapter 19

Lodging

When all your loved ones come into town, they'll need someplace to sleep. Supplying lodging for the out-of-town visitors used to be the bride's family's responsibility, but times have changed and now most guests foot their own bills.

In this short chapter, you'll complete rather quickly the job of booking rooms for your guests, your bridal party, and even yourselves...perhaps at a discount.

Finding lodging for your guests

If your reception will be held at a hotel's banquet hall, then it would make the most sense to book a block of rooms for your guest at that very site. Your banquet hall manager will easily guide you to the selection of a floor and a variety of rooms. Many all-in-one packages come at a discount, and some give the honeymoon suite to the bride and groom for free.

If you're not lucky enough to have the connected reception hall and hotel option, then you'll have to search for the right lodging for your guests. It all depends on the number of people you'll need to host, and the budget level they can afford. Most brides attack this potentially dreadful task by researching hotels at several different budget levels. Although they obviously stay away from the seedy roadside motels with hourly rates, flickering lights, and a "Free HBO" sign, they try to include in their list of possibilities a budget motel that is of high quality.

When searching for a quality hotel in moderate and higher expense brackets, ask the following:

- Is it close to the reception location?
- Does it require complicated travel directions, such as around hard-to-navigate circles?
- Does it have enough rooms?
- What is the nightly price of the rooms?
- Does it have room service? What time do they stop serving?
- Does it offer non-smoking rooms?
- Does it offer cribs and cots?
- Does it offer efficiencies?
- Does it have amenities, such as a spa or workout room, sauna, game room, etc.?
- Is it rated by AAA? How many stars?

When searching for the right place for your guests to stay, you should always tour the hotel in the company of the manager. One bride picked an inexpensive chain hotel that was not far from her reception site and was mortified to hear from her guests that they switched to another hotel because of the original one's dirty rooms and the sighting of a cockroach.

Always inspect a hotel as if you were looking for your own spot to stay. Use your own judgment and request the best for your guests.

When booking the room, be sure to get a solid contract that specifies the number of rooms, the suites you may have selected by name, the floor you want to be on, the date of your guests' arrivals, and your complete contact information. Add the hotel manager's name to your list of pre-wedding confirmation calls, and you're all set.

Package deals

Booking a block of rooms in a hotel's wedding package is not always the best deal. Although you should consider what it offers—such as a champagne breakfast buffet for your guests and your suite for free—be a smart shopper and inspect the package on an itemized basis. Find out what the regular rates for the rooms are on the dates of your wedding weekend. Then itemize your wedding package deal to see what you'll actually save per room. Sometimes, the overfilled package with the seemingly great free services is actually a higher priced collection of what you could get for less in a standard reservation.

Talk to the manager about what is included in the package deal or the group block, and what the deadlines are for booking. Because you'll have to reserve these rooms way in advance on your credit card (remember not to leave this for last minute, as other wedding guests and conference attendees can book up the hotel quickly), a last-minute room count of half might mean that you cannot get your money back. Ask about the refund/cancellation rules and rates, as well as check in and check out times.

Many brides report that their guests loved having a floor or a wing all to themselves, as they could open their doors and socialize to their hearts' content. Having all of your guests in one area also means the noise they make stays in one zone, instead of traveling throughout the hallways.

Part Four

Planning
the
Honeymoon
or Getaway Wedding

Chapter 20

The Honeymoon

Most second-time brides have the luxury of enjoying a longer and more expensive honeymoon than first-time brides. The reason for this trend is that second-time brides are older and more settled in their careers, which means they usually have more vacation time and more money. It's very rare for a 22-year-old bride fresh out of college and starting a new job to get two weeks' vacation time, and she may not have access to an extra $5,000 for a grand tour.

According to a recent survey done by *Bride Again* magazine, here's the breakdown of what brides nationwide are budgeting for their post-wedding getaways:

Under $1,999	14%
$2,000- 2,999	21%
$3,000- 3,999	17%
$4,000- 4,999	25%
$5,000- 7,499	18%
$7,500- 9,999	3%
Over $10,000	2%

With this in mind, you might want to think about how much your wedding budget will affect your vacation plans. Do you want a grand getaway to Europe? Two weeks of island-hopping in Hawaii? Your budget and time allowances will dictate what form your honeymoon plans will take, so look at those sobering facts carefully when considering the possibilities for your honeymoon destination.

The honeymoon destination list

What are second-time brides choosing as the destination for their ultimate getaways? The Caribbean is still the most popular honeymoon (and destination wedding) site, beating out Hawaii by almost 30 percent. "Hawaii is overrun by first-time honeymooners," says one recent second-time bride. "Plus, *I* went there on my first honeymoon, and I want to go someplace different." Perhaps that's why the numbers favor the resorts of the Caribbean, rather than the tropical islands in the Pacific.

Encore couples are also choosing Europe, the Orient, Egypt, Australia, and Canada. These couples report that they want more to do than lie in the sun or scuba dive all day, and they're not interested in some resorts' tendency to resemble a college party scene. They're past their hard drinking stage, and they want to have an adventurous honeymoon with unique activities and photo opportunities. "When would we ever get to Egypt and climb the steps of a temple together? You can't beat that experience, and it's going to be a forever memory," says one groom, thrilled by the arrival of his airline tickets to Cairo. Another says, "We can go to a beach resort anytime."

Also popular are adventure vacations, such as mountain climbs and forest treks. Research these thoroughly, though, as it is a relatively new option in the vacation category, and even some experienced adventure travelers are getting scammed by inferior companies.

The *Bride Again* survey shows that brides and grooms consider the following honeymoon destinations:

The Caribbean	70%
Hawaii	44%
South Pacific	29%
Las Vegas	23%
Mountain resorts	22%
Mexico	19%
Europe	16%
Florida	15%
Canada	4%
Other	11%

The options again are enormous, as you consider that traditionally non-honeymoon spots are now becoming the most popular honeymoon spots for encore couples. The couples I spoke to said they didn't want the same old thing; they wanted a truly exciting and lengthy trip that they could talk about and reminisce about for years.

Some of the more exciting honeymoon destinations reported by the editors of bridal magazines as the hot new spots are:

- Greece.
- Alaska.
- Safaris.
- Mediterranean cruises.
- Australia.
- Fiji.
- The countries of the couple's heritage.

Choosing your style

Stuck on choosing a destination? Do they all sound great to you? Talk with your fiancé about the type of honeymoon you both want. Here are some questions to ask:

1. Do you want or need a relaxing honeymoon, such as a week of uninterrupted lying in the sun?
2. Do you want an active honeymoon, packed with activities?
3. Which kinds of new sports or activities do you want to try on your honeymoon?
4. How far do you want to travel?
5. Do you mind losing a whole day of your honeymoon time on a plane flight?
6. Do you want to go international or stay within the bounds of this country?
7. Which destinations are in season at the time of your wedding?
8. Do you want a honeymoon-type resort or a non-honeymoon-type resort?

The two of you should discuss your preferences and try to incorporate as many of the other's wishes as possible. Some couples split their honeymoons so that, for example, he can have his week of golfing at Hilton Head, and then they both fly down to Mexico so she can have her week of nightlife in Cancun. Your choices may be different, but there is no rule that says you only have to pick one spot.

Family honeymoons—including the kids

The big trend now is planning a family vacation after the wedding. Call it a "family honeymoon" if you will, but it truly is a much-needed getaway for all of you and a chance for you to bond as a complete family now. For some couples, this is the first they've spent extended time together as a whole group, and they find that the time spent traveling and doing fun activities together helps ease the transition and acceptance of stepparents and stepsiblings.

For instance, Daryl and Monica brought their five kids, ranging in age from 12 to 19, to a Las Vegas resort. If you haven't been to Vegas recently, you'll probably be surprised to learn how family-friendly many of the big resorts are now. Daryl and Monica's kids had a blast and actually grew to know each other better. Their initial skepticism about one another faded as they discovered shared interests and talents. From elaborate arcades to shows to indoor amusement parks, aquariums, and tons of places to eat, there's something for everyone, and the energy and excitement are overwhelming.

The "Maui Loves Kids" program in Hawaii provides kids with veritable day-and-night camps, offering programs and activities for children of all ages and ability levels. While you and your new spouse enjoy your romantic sunset walks and days lounging on floating rafts in the ocean, the kids are off biking down volcanoes, learning to snorkel, and searching for starfish. Family time might include a tour through a rainforest—educational for the kids— or a beach luau with hula and fire dancers.

If you're about to combine two families into one, think about the possibilities of this kind of honeymoon. It may be important to your kids to be included so that they don't feel left behind or that you've forgotten about them. They may have been lost in the shuffle as you planned your wedding, and they may fear losing your attention. For many couples, this honeymoon option is the right choice. Talk to your partner about how such a plan fits into your families' schedules, and whether or not your particular brood would mix well for an entire week or longer. You might decide that your kids are just too stubborn right now, and that putting them in a hotel room together might foster arguments and resentments. This is a highly individual situation, and one you must weigh carefully before buying tickets for the kids.

Comparing packages

Whatever style of honeymoon you choose, wherever you go, and whoever is coming along, it's important to make your travel plans carefully. Honeymoon packages come in all shapes and sizes these days, and there are many different plans out there. Again, list what you do and don't want in your honeymoon profile. One tip: Choose a package that is all-inclusive, so all your drinks, meals, and activities are included in one price. This is a popular piece of advice from newly married couples who did not investigate honeymoon or travel packages and wound up paying hundreds of dollars for their bar tab alone. This doesn't make them heavy drinkers, however. Some resorts charge $9 for a piña colada, a high price to pay for that frothy drink of paradise.

If you're not planning on having an active honeymoon, don't choose a package that includes all sporting events. It's wasted money. Instead, match packages to your needs, and itemize the prices to see if you'd spend less by vacationing a la carte.

Ask detailed questions about the size and location of your room or rooms (if you're bringing kids, in which case you should also ask about adjoining rooms). Get layouts of the rooms, not just pictures, and ask how recent those pictures are. Look up all hotels and resorts in popular travel guides, and always call for the most recent travel and pricing information. Internet profiles and magazine articles may be dated, and some international restrictions may have come into play since your particular source was printed. The most recent information is always the best information. Also, get your travel agent's plans in writing, and get copies of all itineraries.

You know how to plan a vacation, and this is an important one. It's one you'll remember forever, time alone with your new spouse and perhaps your new kids. Take special care to make arrangements at only the highest-rated hotels in *safe locales*, and triple-check your plans with confirmation calls before you depart.

Chapter 21

Getaway Weddings

According to Beth Reed Ramirez of *Bride Again* magazine, a full 20 percent of encore brides plan getaway weddings, where their wedding ceremony and honeymoon are held at the same vacation spot. These may be weddings performed by a waterfall in Maui, a ceremony enacted in a town square in the Italian village where your grandparents grew up, a cruise wedding, or even that well-known spectacle of a Las Vegas wedding. Whatever the surroundings, the option of getting married and honeymooning in the same spot is quite attractive to many second-time couples.

Perhaps it's their choice not to do the whole traditional wedding thing in their hometown, but to get the ceremony over with so they can *be* married, rather than *get* married. Many couples don't see the point in devoting such time and expense to the planning of a traditional wedding, when the entire affair can be planned in a few days over the phone with a reputable resort's well-qualified planner taking the helm.

This is not to say that planning a getaway wedding is easier than planning a traditional wedding. In some cases, it may actually be more difficult, such as when dealing with international restrictions, legal marriage rules, and making the best vendor choices from 2,000 miles away. By no means is it always easier, but the effort may be worth it if your particular wedding vision is one in which you'll marry on a Hawaiian beach at sunset with the traditional Hawaiian Wedding Song playing. Or perhaps you're the spontaneous type, and although you'll pay attention to the details in this book as far as your wishes for the many details of your wedding celebration, you might be the type to make a phone call to the Four Seasons in Vegas and jet off a week later to arrive at the wedding of your dreams which has been created as per your requests through their coordinator.

The getaway wedding is gaining in popularity now, and many of the best resorts do offer full-service wedding packages. Their on-staff wedding coordinators handle all of the details, hire all of the best vendors affiliated with the resort, and run the entire event like clockwork. Just be sure to research well, and hire wedding teams at only the best resorts.

You may be able to play the role of wedding coordinator at a destination location on your own, if no resort planner is available, but that option requires researching vendors in all areas, getting referrals from that locale's board of tourism or marriage licensing bureau, interviewing over the phone, requesting press packets, photos, and videos, and planning sight unseen. It has been done successfully by other brides, but they do warn about the intense legwork, the worry caused by planning from afar, and the fears about what will be awaiting them upon their arrival.

In this section, you'll learn about planning a getaway wedding, although I also recommend Denise and Alan Fields' detailed book *Far and Away Weddings*. That book explains the insider secrets to planning from a distant location, and it spotlights several all-inclusive wedding packages at the most popular destination wedding sites around the world. The authors explain how to choose, hire, and work with a destination wedding coordinator, and how to assure the creation of the wedding you want. Their resource list is lengthy, and they provide great tools for planning of your getaway wedding.

Popular getaway wedding sites

Hawaii and the Caribbean top the list of getaway wedding sites. Most of the brides I spoke to said that the idea of doing something different than their first wedding experiences weighed heavily in their plans for this wedding, and they leaned more toward their fantasy getaway visions. They had the money to make their dreams come true, as well.

Other popular destinations for all-inclusive wedding services:

- Napa Valley, California.
- The Disney Resorts (perfect for family getaways).
- Vermont (during foliage and ski seasons).
- Cruises.
- The French Riviera.

Although the specter of international planning and red tape does loom large, couples are embarking upon the detailed work necessary for arranging and legalizing their weddings overseas. It can be done if you follow the guidelines found through that country's tourism board. You'll find many sites listed in the Resources section at the end of this book, so give them a call and ask for an information packet on their wedding offerings.

The legalities

Although planning a destination wedding from 2,000 miles away requires dedication and the partnership of a well-trained on-site planner, you also need to pay attention to the legalities of your destination wedding. We did cover the issue of making your marriage legal in Chapter 6, but I'll reiterate it here so that you know what implications your legal needs impose on the wedding plans. Again, you'll want to make sure your wedding is not only beautiful and well-documented, but also completely valid in the eyes of church and state:

1. Call the location's board of marriage licensing to request their current requirements. Do not take the information listed in dated brochures or on the Internet as gospel, as rules change every day.
2. Find out what blood and medical tests are needed, as well as whether or not tests taken in your home state will be legal at the site of the wedding. Some countries and islands require that you get your blood tests done within their territories. If this is the case, ask for the waiting period and effectiveness period.
3. Find out what kinds of identification you need. You might need to bring along copies of your birth certificates, driver's licenses, divorce papers, or death certificates from your first marriages.
4. Get a written copy of your officiant's license to perform ceremonies.
5. Get your wedding package contract written out fully and sent to you, signed by the wedding coordinator at the site of your intended nuptials.
6. Confirm several months, weeks, and days in advance.

The guest list

A big trend in getaway weddings now is the inclusion of a small group of close family and friends. Although you may decide to fly off on your own, just the two of you, to be married on a Martinique beach, consider the idea of bringing your immediate family and best friends out to the island or on the cruise to participate in your wedding. Very often, this makes the ceremony and celebration more special, as you'll share it with the most important people in your lives. Most brides I spoke to said they loved having their parents, siblings, nieces, nephews, and friends in attendance at their faraway weddings, and everyone enjoyed the change of scenery and lavish vacation.

Group getaways can encompass an entire week's worth of activities for your entire entourage, which makes for an enjoyable wedding celebration for all. One guest invited on a weekend cruise wedding raved about the experience, saying that if she ever married again that's how she would plan her future event. "We had a group of 20," she said. "And we had a *blast!* The wedding part was lovely, simple, and fitting for the bride and groom's style, and then we all just partied for the rest of the weekend. It was a great trip!"

Before you announce your plans and invite your guests on the getaway, though, consider the realities. Will you be paying for your guests' travel and lodging? You should, as it is unfair to impose that kind of expense on your loved ones just because you want them there. Consider that travel and lodging for your guests is a small percentage of the usual budget of a large, traditional wedding, and offer to pick up your guests' tabs in your all-inclusive plan. Talk with your on-site wedding coordinator ahead of time, and arrange for a one-price, all-inclusive arrangement for your guests so that you don't have to police their bar tabs or room service orders. This forethought will save you money and stress, so keep it in mind.

Give your guests at least three months' notice before your planned getaway wedding, so that they can arrange for vacation time and find sitters for the kids. Be considerate of others' work and school schedules, and make use of holiday weekends and school vacations.

Be specific about who is invited, so that married couples don't assume that their teenagers are invited too, if that's the case. Diplomatically explain your constraints in both budget and space to your guest, and be clear about the invitation list.

Be considerate of your guests' needs and preferences. If your mother is afraid to fly, don't pressure her to get on a plane to come to Hawaii with you. That request may be traumatic for her, and she may resent your muscling her into facing a fear she's not ready to deal with yet. If your brother-in-law is struggling to overcome a gambling addiction, don't plan a Vegas wedding. Be thoughtful of your guests' needs, and always see if there are activities and offerings at your getaway wedding site to interest everyone in your group. You'll need some time alone with your new spouse after the wedding, so be sure the rest of your clan has a full schedule to keep them busy.

Part Five

Countdown to the Wedding

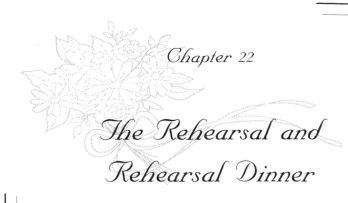

Chapter 22

The Rehearsal and Rehearsal Dinner

A ll the major plans for the wedding are set, and now it's time to arrange the choreography of your day, making sure that all the involved parties know what they are do to, when they are to do it, where they are to go, what they are to say, when to sit, and when to stand. For most brides and grooms, this is a very exciting time. It's when they see their vision begin to come together. All of their loved ones are gathered together—perhaps for the first time in this whole planning process—and the excitement of the upcoming event is evident.

A good rehearsal is highly organized, swift and efficient, and answers all possible questions. If you have a wedding coordinator, she's done this many, many times, and she knows how to speed the process along in a complete manner, instructing all without being a drill sergeant, and laying the foundation for a seamless flow of events on the wedding day. All of your questions will be answered before you even have a chance to think them up.

If you'll be married in a traditional religious setting, the priest, pastor, or rabbi will also be well-versed in instructing the members of your party and all participants. The rehearsal there too may be quick, painless, and complete.

But what happens if you are without a traditional priest or an organized coordinator? What happens if it's all up to *you?* After all, you wanted your wedding planned to your specifications, you've worked hard to put the whole thing together, and now you're the leader. *You* are the choreographer. You have 20 people wandering around your backyard, a garden, or a historical site, looking to you to find out what's expected of them.

Don't panic. With the information you'll find out right here, you will be every bit as organized and well-versed as a highly experienced wedding coordinator. You'll address every issue efficiently, and you'll handle the many diplomacy situations with ease and the skill of a family therapist. Best of all, most second-time brides agree, you truly do get to create your wedding day. You're not at the mercy of the whims or creative vision of a coordinator or stylist, and you are not bound by the dictates of a formal, traditional wedding.

Because I do not know your individual situation, I've combined approaches in this chapter. The question lists can either be asked of a planner or considered and answered by you. That's the beauty of this section. Take the time now, before the rehearsal day, to think over these issues, plan ahead, see what you want, and be ready to put every piece into place when the planning process comes to this last crucial step.

Running the show

No matter who is officially in charge of running the rehearsal, you are still the ultimate authority. It's your wedding, and you get to say what you want and don't want. You may think back to your first wedding, when the officiant or planner just physically placed people in line, you walked through the processional, were told vague descriptions of what would happen when, and then marched back up the aisle on your fiancé's arm. It was all rushed and cookie-cutter, and you really didn't have much say in the matter.

Well, now it's different. As an encore bride, perhaps with the wisdom and strength of age, you'll undoubtedly feel more comfortable about asking questions or saying quite simply, "No, that's not what I had in mind." You're not the deer caught in the headlights that you may have been at your first wedding, and you're not going to be led by the shoulder to where you'll stand or how you'll make your entrance.

It's important to begin thinking about the rehearsal by affirming to yourself your role as the creator of this ceremony. You have the right to speak up. You have the right to question. You have the right to make changes at the last minute. It's all within your power to do so.

That said, let's tackle the planning of your rehearsal.

Getting everyone in line

When your attendants and ceremony participants arrive at the ceremony site, there will be a lot of mingling, chit-chatting, and excited energy. You can't avoid this, so don't waste your energy expecting everyone to be all business from moment one. Allow everyone to socialize, make introductions where necessary, and give them a good 15 to 20 minutes to get acquainted or make small talk if they haven't seen each other for a while. Let them get it out of their system. Brides who haven't given their bridal parties some free assembling time at the outset report that their attendants were distracted during the instructional part of the rehearsal. Perhaps they were talking amongst themselves, not taking the event very seriously.

You will avoid this problem by letting them loose to relax with one another, get some of the buzz out of their system, and—yes, it will happen—check out that attractive usher they haven't met yet. Bridal parties are notorious for that, as you well know.

Then, start the process by getting everyone's attention. Gather everyone to you, and set the standard for the rehearsal by spelling out what you need right then. Try this: "Everyone, we're ready to start." (Your group gathers in close, smiles on their faces.) "Okay, thanks for being here on time. We're ready to start. First of all, you'll be happy to know that this is not going to take long at all." (Your group will be happy to know the parameters.) "I need you all to give your undivided attention as we run through the steps of the ceremony twice." (Let them know what to expect.) "Please be sure to ask any questions you have, as we want to make sure you're all clear on what's expected of you. So now, let's get started so we can get out of here and get to the rehearsal dinner!"

Your upbeat mood is important. Yes, you may be nervous, even if this is your third time down the aisle, but it's your demeanor that sets the stage for a successful and complete rehearsal. If you're terrified, barking orders, or stressing out, your attendants will be uneasy. And that's not the best way to get things done. Just relax, smile, share in the celebratory mood, and start the rehearsal off in the most advantageous way.

Unfortunately, though, this is not a perfect world. You may have immature ushers who are not paying attention. You may have sour-grapes bridesmaids sulking through the processional. You may have a problem child as a ring-bearer, and the tantrums are throwing everyone off. Many brides have stories like these, and they share with you their universal advice: Ignore the negative attitudes of those who intend to bring you down.

If you don't respond, if you stay happy and focus on the joy of the event, they don't get what they want. Immature ushers should be quietly confronted and asked to act their age. Tantrum-prone kids...well, just get through it. That's the chance any bride takes. Overall, the best you can do is encourage your attendants and participants to take the rehearsal seriously, and if they do not comply, *they* will look foolish on the big day.

One step at a time

The first step is instructing the ushers about seating. Yours may not be an ultra-formal affair where the ushers are to escort the women down an aisle and seat them according to a personalized chart. If that is the case, the ushers need to know what their duties will be. Remember, many of them have been ushers before, and they may be used to the more traditional ways of seating guests. Again, you must specify. Many, many brides and grooms regret not taking the time to give clear, emphasized instructions to their ushers at the rehearsal. With the many strains of family dynamics, which always seem to lead to volcanic blowups about who is ranked where in the family and who is slighting whom, wedding ceremony seating is actually a very big deal. Guests do get upset if they feel snubbed in favor of the groom's side, and so on. It's rather petty, but it does put a pall on a wedding day. So give the ushers detailed instructions about who is to be seated where. You have no idea the headaches you'll avoid if this is done well.

The second step is arranging the processional. Your bridesmaids and maid or matron of honor will be lined up in the order you've chosen, and they will be led to where they will wait for the processional. If you are in a church, it will be the entrance hall. If you are in a home, it may be an upstairs room, ready for descent down an ornate flight of stairs. If there is no processional, and the bridal party will simply take their places where the ceremony will be performed, instruct them on that as well. The women will need to know the path they will be taking, the timing of their approach, the space you want between them, and where they stand or sit.

The men will also need to know whether or not they are part of the processional, where they stand if they will not be escorting the women down the aisle, and whether they stand or sit at the outset of the processional. The same goes for child attendants.

Next is the most important part: your approach. Again, you may be taking a special walk down a flight of stairs adorned with garlands of greenery, roses, and white lights. You may be walking down a cobblestone path in a lush, fragrant garden filled with white daisies and lavender. Whatever your setting, be sure that you have good footing. Put on the shoes that you're planning to wear at the wedding, and see how well you can handle the walk. You don't want to be stiff and fearful of losing traction on a stairway, and you don't want to break a heel on rough cobblestone. Some brides have actually changed their footwear to flats because they learned at their reception sites that their heels sank into the ground on every step. These kinds of small details are the brilliant, damage-control saves of successful rehearsals.

Time your entrance, instruct your bridal party as to what to do when you approach, and take your walk toward your groom.

At your first wedding, you were probably given away by your father. Now, as a second-time bride, you can choose any of the following options:

- Walking down the aisle by yourself, choosing to not be given away by anyone.
- Walking down the aisle with your groom.
- Walking down the aisle with your child or children.
- Walking down the aisle with your father and stepfather, if you have equal relationships with both.
- Walking down the aisle with both your parents.
- Walking down the aisle with your mother.

All options are open to you. Some brides have "stations;" their father walks them to a certain point, then their closer stepfather, and then the groom walks them the rest of the way. The important thing is to be sure you are comfortable with the arrangement. Many second-time brides with children love the idea of having their kids escort them down the aisle. They share a special moment with the kids, they're all a big focal point, they get a large dose of attention as cameras snap away, and the kids are an important inclusion in the ceremony. Whatever you choose, practice the procedure now.

Going through the ceremony

It is a good idea to run through the basics of the ceremony with the officiant. This way, you get to be sure the officiant will follow your instructions for the ceremony, and you get a run-through yourselves of what will come when. After all, you will not have a copy of the program in your hands, and you will need a reminder of what will be expected of you.

When the time arrives, have the musicians perform their songs. Take the time now to do this, as they will need to adjust their sound to the surroundings. It will only take a few minutes, and the bridal party will love hearing the music you've chosen. It adds to the excitement and feeling of preparation for the day.

You should also have those who will be doing readings for you practice their speeches. This gives them a chance to work through some nerves, not "read cold" on the wedding day, and also adjust their sound to suit the microphone or the acoustics of the room or open-air area.

Recite your vows. Again, this avoids the "cold reading," gives you a practice run, and adds to the celebration. If, like some couples, you don't want to reveal the entirety of your vows before the big day, you can choose to read just the first few sentences.

Many couples choose to have their children participate in the ceremony. It means a lot to them, as a sign of including the children in the importance of the union, and it gives the children a chance to shine. In Chapter 7, you read about asking your children what they would like to do during the ceremony, what their roles might be. They may have agreed to do a reading or be a part of the ring exchange. Do *not* be surprised if your children change their minds now. This happens all the time. Remember, children have a hard time coping with change, and although they may have been happy about your wedding plans a few months ago, they're facing reality now. This wedding is really upon them, and they may be dealing with some tough feelings.

If they balk at being readers, or if they are belligerent about being a part of the service, it may not come out until the rehearsal. You may have seen their moodiness, but the actual revolt may get spurred on by the immediacy of the rehearsal, the final sign that you are indeed marrying someone else. If your children refuse or makes a scene—which has happened—promise yourself that you will handle it in the best way possible. Do not rebuke your children in front of the crowd. Be understanding, not only of their transitional feelings, but also of their ages. They may be resisting for any number of reasons, including the fear of being the center of attention. Do not try to read their minds, and do not try to sway them to your needs. The worst thing you could do is lash out with, "Are you trying to ruin my wedding?" If you have kids, it's their wedding too, and your children should not be forced to participate against their wishes. Respect them and yourself enough by taking them aside, asking them why they've changed their minds, and then accepting their wishes. They do not have to join in the service if it's against their will, even if it's printed in the program that they will. Simply excuse them from responsibility for this event, and be calm about finding a replacement. This is no time for a fight. It all will work out fine.

Go over the exchange of rings, using rings other than the real wedding bands for this practice run, and take the time to practice your kiss. Some couples report that their first kiss, as viewed by so many, was actually a disappointment! "I was going for the quick smooch, and he went for the longer, more passionate kiss," says Ellen, who was married last year on a beach in Cape Cod. "What resulted was an awkward kiss, which we tried to cover up by going for another kiss, and everyone joked around, saying 'What, you've never kissed her before?' It was a downer." So practice that kiss, even if it seems unromantic to do so. Agree on your wedding day kiss style.

The recessional

This one is a cinch. It should be practiced, though, because you may choose to have your kids walk with you down the aisle, as a family. Teach the bridal party about pairing up for their walk back, especially if you have an odd number of attendants and you'll need to pair one man up with two women, or vice versa.

Last details

Of course, you may choose to have your ushers double back and indicate the recessional order of the guests. Simply inform them to go back to the first row and keep the guests flowing out of their seats toward you.

Establishing a receiving line is up to you. That's mainly a first-wedding thing, a formality, and many brides report hating having to stand in a line and get only a few seconds with each guest as they get rushed through the lineup. Instead, follow the advice of other brides and skip the receiving line. You'll be mingling with all of the guests throughout the reception.

Before you break away for the rehearsal dinner, ask if your bridal party members have any questions, need any more clarification, or have any problems with the elements of the ceremony. One bride reports that her Protestant bridesmaid was not sure what to do during the Roman Catholic communion procession. Should she swallow the wafer? Just shake her head no when the priest offers it to her? That bride was happy that her bridesmaid spoke up and addressed a major problem, one that applied to other members of the bridal party as well. A short discussion ensued, and the officiant learned how to handle the non-Catholic participants. Compare that to the one bridesmaid in a different wedding who didn't know what to do with the wafer and stuck it in her bouquet. The guests were shocked and dismayed, and that one act was the talk of the reception.

Now that all of the details are addressed and everyone has directions and instructions, it's time to head off for the rehearsal dinner.

The rehearsal dinner

Rehearsal dinners are almost always very relaxed and informal. Many second-time brides choose to forego the buffet and "mini-wedding" that they may have had the first time around in favor of a large table at a favorite family restaurant. Other rehearsal dinner options you might consider are the following:

- A catered dinner at home.
- An informal dinner at home, with your family's favorite lasagna and meatballs, some great wine, and a few loaves of bread.
- A brunch after a morning rehearsal.
- A wine and cheese party at a winery.
- A backyard barbecue.
- A picnic by the lake.
- A clambake at the beach.

Wherever you choose to hold your rehearsal dinner, make sure it is relaxed and different from the wedding day style and menu. This makes the event stand out, and it allows your bridal party and participants to unwind and celebrate your upcoming marriage in a more intimate way.

Proposing toasts

This is the time for proposing toasts. Anyone can do it. Even children of the bride and groom have given speeches and proposed toasts to Mom and Dad. You and the groom may choose to give a little talk about your relationship and what you mean to each other. One groom touched the hearts of everyone in attendance as he stood at the front of the room and said the following to the 14-year-old girl who would become his stepdaughter the next day: "Vanessa, tomorrow I will promise to be a faithful, loving husband to your mother. I love her more than anything, and I'm so grateful

I found her. But tonight, I'm promising in front of all these people and from the bottom of my heart that I will always be a faithful, loving stepfather to you. I know you love your father, and I agree he's done a wonderful job raising you. But I add my love and support to your life as well, promising that I will always be there for you no matter what you need."

Aside from these amazing family moments, shared only in the company of close friends and relatives, there may be a fair amount of joking, optimistic speculation about the wedding day, and a little bragging about how great your cake is going to be.

The big gift exchange

Give your attendants, your children, your parents, and each other the special gifts you have chosen just for them, and watch the joy begin to spread as everyone admires your good taste.

This is the time to give your kids a family medallion to be worn on the wedding day. The medallions you will find on the market are very popular, and they come in different styles. You'll find more information on these in Chapter 25 and in the Resources section.

Rehearsal dinner do's and don'ts

Do's:

1. Allow guests to mingle. Let your bridal party get to know each other.
2. Plan on easy food preparation if you will be cooking. A big lasagna (half with meat and half without), store-bought stuffed shells, or trays of sloppy joe sandwiches are always an enjoyable menu, and you don't have to spend the whole night watching what's in the oven or standing over the stove.
3. Provide food choices your kids like too. A wine and cheese party may be great for you, but what will your kids eat and drink?
4. Enlist setup and cleanup help from others.
5. Decorate with fresh flowers, candles, and other minimal-effort items.
6. Propose a toast to your partner.
7. Propose a toast to your kids.
8. Videotape the entire thing, and take pictures.

Don'ts:

1. Try to plan a mini-wedding. This doesn't have to be a big, impressive meal.
2. Get drunk. You don't want anyone hung over for the wedding day.
3. Allow people to ask for changes in the wedding plans. Some people may try to pipe in at the last minute, asking for some addition to the ceremony or some adherence to old-fashioned etiquette. Simply smile, say the plans are set, and change the subject.
4. Advertise how stressed out you are. Just enjoy the moment. The still-to-be-dealt-with details can be done later.
5. Stay up too late. Get good sleep for the next day. You will need it.

Chapter 23

Bridal Beauty

Of course, you'll want to look your best on your wedding day. After all, you'll be the center of attention, the focus of many adoring eyes and cameras, and your look will be captured in your photos and wedding video. Best of all is the sense of pampering you'll get when talented stylists get your hair, makeup, and nails just right, and you've been pampered and primped for your shining moment.

You may think all you have to do is make hair, nail, and makeup appointments for the wedding morning, but the smartest brides prepare their looks way in advance. They practice with different styles, different shades, and different looks until they find the one that's perfect for the wedding they've planned and that's also perfect for them. So think ahead, make some appointments now, tell your stylists that you're experimenting for your wedding day, and enjoy the repeated makeovers until you find the looks that are just perfect.

Hair

Unless your hair is very short, you have a lot of options for how you can wear it on your wedding day. It all really depends upon the gown you've chosen, and if you've followed my advice earlier, you considered your hairdo—down or upswept—when you were trying on gowns or dresses. Now, it's time for the fun stuff, the practicing of hairstyles. Do you want your hair blown straight for a sleek, elegant look, perhaps pinned up in a chignon?

Do you envision yourself with a loose, flowing, curly, tendril-style 'do? Consider your options, know what looks good on you and what doesn't, and then find a good hairstylist who can practice various styles on you.

Your stylist is going to need to know some information first:

- What does your gown look like?
- What is the formality of your wedding?
- What is the style of your wedding?
- Will it be outdoors, so that you have to face humidity or wind?
- What is your face shape?
- What style suits your age?

Your stylist will professionally assess your hair, your body shape, the neckline of your dress, and all of the other factors that work with finding the correct hairstyle for you. If you will be outdoors on a humid day, your stylist will know what kind of upsweep will work best and which products will prevent the frizzies. You'll have to have an honest discussion with her, so that you can start the process with all of the pertinent info. Taking these steps now will ensure that your hair complements your look on your wedding day, and that it doesn't fall apart or look like it belongs on someone else's body.

Nikki Padula of the Minardi Salon in New York City suggests keeping a natural look to your hair. A fiercely-hairsprayed french braid may look too solid on you, and you'll have to chip it apart after the wedding. Even if your hairstyle is upswept and needs a mist of hairspray, your stylist should be able to recommend and use a more natural, powerful-hold hairspray that is not like shellac. Your hair should be touchable, soft, and elegant. Upswept curls and twists should be smooth and gel-free. One of the best and most versatile styles that works with most formalities and weather conditions is the half-upsweep, where half of the hair is pinned up, and some falls down in tendrils or smooth wisps. This style is low-maintenance, brings out the eyes, allows a view of the jewelry, and works with most necklines.

As a second-time bride, you'll most likely be skipping the veil. Some encore brides are using a headpiece veil, but the vast majority are going with tiaras or flowers tucked into loosely twisted hair, or they are letting their own gently-sculpted hair be the focal point. Padula suggests trying out a tiara or headpiece with loose, flowing hair for a natural look. You can get pretty, inexpensive tiaras from accessory shops at the mall, rather than dropping a few thousand on a diamond-studded tiara from a department store counter. The styles available now are studded with gentle faux pearls and blush-colored stones and pieces, and they work very well for a classic look.

There is no limit to the amount of hairstyles you can try. Simply book a stylist for a few hours and experiment with styles and shapes that complement your look.

For healthy hair, which is essential, follow these tips:

1. Clean and moisturize as needed. Some hair specialists say that it's a bad idea to condition your hair every day, as that may strip your hair of its natural oils.
2. Find the best shampoo and conditioner for your style and hair type.
3. Get hair colored two to three weeks before the wedding. Don't try a new color, and don't try difficult processes on your own. Dye your hair on your own only if you've always done so, otherwise go to a pro.
4. Don't try new haircuts or color designs. This is not the time for a great new cut that might have you bawling a few hours later, and it's not the time to try out the new razor-trimming styles, color blocking, and other procedures.
5. Start growing your hair out when you first get engaged. The longer your hair, the more options you will have.
6. Get regular trims every six to eight weeks.
7. Use deep moisturizing products as specified on the box or bottle.
8. Look for products that add shine to hair without making it look oily.

Makeup

Your wedding-day makeup will depend greatly on what your personal makeup style is. You would be best served to stick with the makeup you always use, adding some well-placed enhancement to bring out your best features. I advise using your own makeup, as your skin is used to it. Trying out a new brand may cause skin irritations, and it may be hard to find the perfect match to your skin tone. With your own supply, you know your skin is comfortable with it and you know the colors that work well on you.

It's important to look like yourself on your wedding day. If your regular look is more natural, you won't want to make your grand entrance made up like you're ready for a Broadway stage, with fake eyelashes, bright red lips, and distracting pearlized lavender eye shadow. Stick with your natural look, and just put a little more emphasis on blush, eyeliner, and lipstick.

Makeup pros and photographers alike say that a more pronounced makeup look makes brides look better in their photos, and it does give them a more glamorous look for the big day.

It's a great idea to practice your look with a makeup artist a few months before the big day. She can tell you about the big new colors and which tones are right for your face and your accessories, and she can expertly apply makeup that can bring out your eyes in a whole new way. "I've been applying my own makeup since I was 13 years old," says Victoria. "But when the makeup artist did it, I was amazed that she could make my cheekbones look so much better just by applying blush in a different way. It was humbling to need makeup lessons at my age, but I was grateful for the instruction, as I looked amazing on my wedding day...and every day after."

Most second-time brides do hire makeup artists for at least a makeup consultation, if not for a full application on the day of the wedding. Barbara Stone, a makeup stylist at Bobbi Brown's studio in New York City, recommends visiting a professional, well-trained makeup artist for instruction and product recommendation, even if your budget does not allow for the wedding-day makeup session.

Makeup artist Laura Gellar adds that if you will be using a makeup artist on your wedding day, consider getting the same service for all of your bridesmaids. Ask the stylist how many hair and makeup designers her company has available, and price them for an hour or so of makeovers in the morning. Many second-time brides love this option, as it may be a change from what they experienced during their first marriage. Most said they simply went to a nearby salon, got a French twist and manicure, and came home to dress. With this option, the makeup artists come to you. They set up their makeup mirrors and lay out their tools in your home, and you sit back, relaxed, getting the movie star treatment. It's a popular option, and one that many brides suggest.

"One of the greatest benefits of hiring makeup artists to come to the house was that my 15-year-old daughter, my 13-year-old stepdaughter, and their two friends were given the royal treatment," says Brandi, a recent bride. "It really set them at ease for the rest of the day, as they glowed with self-confidence and soaked in all of the compliments they received. I had the photographer take lots of pictures of them, and they felt like movie stars. It was a great gift for them, and a great start to the day. The girls bonded over that, which actually helped us to combine our family more."

One other thing to consider when dealing with makeup stylists is whether their personal style is in line with yours. Tell them how you wear your makeup, show them pictures, and ask them to use a light hand and avoid overly dramatic lines and shades. They too need to know the details of the wedding, whether or not it will be outdoors in natural light, and what the formality will be. They too will need to tailor your look to suit your tastes and the event itself. So practice well with a variety of makeup stylists until you find the right one.

As for the general rules of wedding day makeup, consider this quality advice from many makeup experts:

1. Use the right foundation. Check it out in regular, indoor lighting and outside in the sun. Be sure it gives even coverage, and does not look caked-on. If your foundation is too heavy, as some are, it will make you look older. So experiment ahead of time to find a good foundation if your regular type is too heavy for your style of wedding.

2. Use waterproof mascara, for obvious reasons.

3. Use lip liner. It keeps your lipstick from bleeding, and it gives a nice, finished look.

4. Use the right shade of pressed powder throughout the day to keep away shiny foreheads and noses. Those dewy moments come through in pictures as an oily face, so you want to make sure you are regularly powdered to keep away more glow than you want.

5. Use a little bit more blush than you usually apply. A good stylist can help you apply it well, and in the right shade for your face. You don't want overly bright stripes on the side of your face. The trick is to look better in the pictures, but not like a clown in person.

6. Take it easy on the glitter. Some brides are using the currently popular body glitter to bring a radiant look to their skin, but I've seen some over-application that was not pretty. If you'd like to use a body mist glitter application like that available from Victoria's Secret, keep in mind that less is more.

7. Check for lipstick on your teeth throughout the day and night.

8. Check for other people's lipstick smears on your cheeks from all of those relatives' kisses.

9. Clear out corners of eyes from time to time throughout the night. Your makeup will travel into those spots as time goes by, and no one is going to point those clumps out to you—except me. So during bathroom breaks, clean out those corners.

Nails

Hands down, the most popular nail style for weddings is the French manicure, both for hands and feet. You may go for that clean, elegant look, or your may choose to add a splash of blush color to your nails, especially if your gown is of color. Again, visit your manicurist to see which shades she has, bring in a swatch of your gown, and try out several options for your big day.

Avoid the following nail no-no's for wedding days:

1. Nix the very long nails. You may be fond of your extra-long nails, but they can look like harsh talons, and they can run stockings and delicate gown material. Cut them down to a shorter, uniform length for the best appearance.
2. Get a professional manicure on the big day. If you plan to do it yourself, you may have shaky hands and a less-than-perfect nail job.
3. No polish in extreme colors.
4. No nail decor, such as nail art or jeweled applications.
5. Avoid the too natural look, such as a simple coating of clear polish. You do want your hands to look "finished," so choose a blush color or French manicure for the right touch.
6. Be sure to have your toenails done as well. Even if you'll be wearing closed-toe shoes for the wedding, you still may be barefoot for the honeymoon, and well-groomed toes will look great.
7. Get the full pedicure. The soaking and sloughing process will get rid of calluses and dry skin on the backs and bottoms of your heels.

Skin

Healthy skin is beautiful skin, and you'll radiate good looks through the care of your skin. You've always known to apply sunscreen and moisturizer as part of your daily care, to use a good cleanser and to take off your makeup before bed each night, right? Now, with as much time as you have before the wedding, you can pamper your skin for that healthy, lovely glow. If you are going to try new products, just be sure to start several months before the wedding, so you don't risk skin irritations and breakouts before the big day.

All skin experts agree that the steps to good skin are cleansing, exfoliating, moisturizing, and protecting. Choose your products with care, get a good skin care expert to recommend the right products for you, and—most importantly—take your own steps to care for your skin. In addition to applying the right cleansers and creams, you'll encourage healthy skin by incorporating the following smart skin-care practices:

- Drink plenty of water. Hydrated skin is less dry and healthier.
- Get plenty of sleep. The body's cells need sleep to replenish, and a lack of sleep gives you those dark, aging circles under your eyes.
- Get plenty of exercise. Exercise, you know, is good for your heart and your body, but it also brings a healthy glow to your skin.
- Use sunscreen. Yes, we all feel like we look better with a tan, but the damage to your skin is not worth it. Avoid tanning beds, as some intensifier creams can burn the living daylights out of you.
- Avoid self-tanners. Some people get good results, but if you're not well-practiced, you don't want to be an orange-streaked mess.
- Use moisturizers at night. Invest in a good nighttime skin cream and apply it according to directions.
- Use wrinkle-erasing creams. I swear by L'Oreal Plenitude Line Eraser Daily Treatment.
- Use under-eye creams. If you have dark circles or puffy bags under your eyes, start a solid, regular regimen of applying a quality under-eye cream. I recommend the proven Vita-K Solution gel.
- Moisturize your lips. Dry, chapped lips can split and crack, and at certain times of year, your lips will be drier than others. Moisturize well.
- Apply foot moisturizer and then cotton socks at night.
- Moisturize your hands. They will be on display.
- Moisturize your decolletage and neck. They too will be on view, and it's a good idea to start a skin care regime for these areas now.

Waxing, trimming, plucking, and other joys

A good eyebrow shaping can open up your whole face. You may be adept at handling your usual eyebrow shape for the day-to-day routines of your life, but you might choose to hire an eyebrow shaper to get the arch and shape just right. It is a bit of an added expense, but the trend right now is for the *full* beauty treatment, including brow shaping.

As for waxing, I know, it's never fun, but it is a crucial element to your wedding day preparation. Spend a few weeks growing out your bikini line (and some brides say your underarms as well, if you can hide the growth from all you know), so that you can get a really great, complete waxing at your salon. Bikini, French, and Brazilian waxing are all the rage now, and a good waxing job will make sure you don't have to do any touch-ups on your honeymoon. You may choose to have your upper lip waxed, as well as your calves, thighs, and any other trouble spots. The little pain now is worth the clean look, and it will save you effort during the weeks after your wedding.

Massage

You know that a massage is great for when you just can't take the pressure anymore, but did you know that massage has proven health benefits? It lowers blood pressure, relaxes knotted muscles that contribute to back, neck, and shoulder pain, and it produces the body's feel-good hormones.

At some points during the planning process, especially if your planning is turning up battles and power struggles, you would be wise to find a good day spa (at *www.spafinder.com*) and book yourself a nice half-hour massage. The best massage therapists use scented oils or creams, play relaxing music, light candles, and employ a relaxing touch. It's a half-hour break from planning and from the tension of your every day life.

Of course, spas offer more than massages, and some offer bridal packages that are amazing deals for you and your bridal party. Consider the offerings, never book unusual spa treatments for the day before the wedding (you don't know what that seaweed wrap will do to your skin), and book your massage, manicure, pedicure, hair, and nails at a relaxing salon where you may even be served breakfast and mimosas. Brides who have booked this type of outing, sharing the pampering with their bridal parties and kids, say that the getaway was a wonderful way to start the day. Some brides say they just took their stepdaughters with them for the full package, as that was more within their budget, and the "girls' day out" was a fun bonding experience.

Pampering for the groom

He may not be up for the herbal wraps, the guy-manicure, or even a back waxing, but he certainly will need a good haircut a few days before the wedding, and a close shave. He may resist the spa treatment, and you'll need to trust him to do his own grooming, no matter how you feel about that goatee or that beard.

At the very least, sign him up for a good massage, or use what you've learned at your own kneading sessions to loosen him up!

Chapter 24

Time Out From Planning

Most brides face a large amount of stress when dealing with all of the many aspects of the wedding planning process. First-time brides have to deal with navigating unfamiliar territory in the bridal industry, dealing with professionals and terminology they may not know very well. They may clash with their in-control parents, or just simply worry about every little detail. You, on the other hand, may have it even worse.

Not only do you have to handle all of the various wedding planning details, but you may have to deal with added pressures from family relationships, strained acceptance from your groom's side of the family, negative attitudes from those who have issues of their own about remarriage, and surly teenage children who may not be quite accepting of this blending of their families. And what about your ex? Your ex's new partner? Your own jitters and fears? At certain times, you may want to just step away from the entire thing, and so you should.

Planning a wedding is always a stressful event, especially when you add in emotions and unknowns and family dynamics, not just for you but for your partner and your kids. I have always advised brides to avoid making their weddings their whole lives, to be able to step away and decompress with some other topic and activity so that the wedding itself does not eclipse what is supposed to be a happy, joyous time in your lives. When things get tense, it's time for some stress relief, some escape, and some self-nurturing so that you can recharge and handle the rest of the planning in a strong and healthy way. So keep the following stress-buster ideas in mind, either for you or for anyone else involved in the planning.

Good health

The only way to handle all of life's situations is to take good care of yourself and maintain your own health. Your body and mind are connected, and stress can cause any number of physical maladies from stomach upsets, headaches, even allergy attacks. Draining your system means you will not only look haggard, but you will not have the stamina you need to handle all of the details of your life, not just the details of the wedding. You must maintain at this time your ability to not only plan the wedding, but also to do your job, handle your household, and raise your kids. I'll keep these suggestions short, as you've no doubt read about them in magazines and books, but they are worth a mention.

Get plenty of sleep

I've suggested this in the previous chapter about good skin care, but your body needs sleep for more than just a rosy glow and the absence of dark circles under your eyes. The mind needs a good eight hours of solid sleep so that it can function well. Without enough sleep, your brain does not function at optimum capacity. Medical studies have been done on sleep-deprived patients, and doctors have found that lack of sleep causes physical distress to the body and hampers decision-making ability. It impedes your memory, and you will need to remember all of the ins and outs of your wedding plans. Lack of sleep can make you irritable, it can affect your ability to handle stress, and it can make you a generally unpleasant person to be with. So be sure to get your eight hours. Schedule them in. Go to bed early if you have to. Consider it mind health, and do not try to run on five hours of sleep and a gallon of coffee. You're not more alert that way. You're just faking alertness, and your mind will catch up to you. Give sleep its due, and get your shut-eye.

Nutrition

The most harried people today do not eat very well. The instant ups of coffee and sweets may get you charged, but then you sink lower than you felt before. Your body needs healthy foods to function optimally, and with a well-rounded diet full of fruits and vegetables, lean meats, fish, grains, and healthy snacks, you will feel better. It may be too much to ask of you to take on a whole new diet, but it would be worth your while for your own benefit and for your family's to incorporate more healthy foods into your menu.

Too many brides try to diet their way into a size 6 wedding gown during the months before their wedding, but you're older and wiser, and you know not to do that. Diet shakes just give you the shakes. Starvation and fierce restriction are a no-no. Eat well, treat yourself every now and then, but be sure you are fueling your body the right way instead of with quick artificial fixes.

Another part of good nutrition is taking quality multi-vitamins. If you haven't already started on this path, ask your pharmacist to recommend a good brand and formula of vitamins for you. Check out One a Day's Web site for a complete list of the different types of formulas, such as extra calcium, antioxidant, and so on at *www.oneaday.com*. The body needs its regular fix of vitamins in addition to the good, nutritious foods you eat, and a multivitamin is a nice treat for it.

What are you drinking?

Again, we've already talked about the importance of drinking water for your skin's health and radiance, but it's also a good idea to drink lots of water for your body's health. Dehydration does affect the rest of the body's functioning. It affects your hair, your skin, your nails, your digestion, and even your mind process. Carry a large bottle of spring water with you everywhere you go, and be sure you're getting plenty of water into your system.

If you're a big soda, iced tea, tea, or coffee drinker, now is not the time to go cold turkey on cutting out caffeine. Although it is a smart health idea to limit the amount of caffeine you get, you have enough to deal with right now without trying to give up what amounts to an addiction. Just limit your caffeinated drinks as much as possible, alternate with water or with non-caffeinated iced teas and teas, and try to remember the body's need for healthier sources of energy.

I can't bring myself to advise you to avoid alcohol. But I can ask you to limit it. At the end of a long, stressful day of planning, work, bickering with florists, and defending your position on the etiquette "breaches" your mother-in-law has scouted out of some antiquated book, you may need to just sit back in a comfy chair with a glass of Merlot. A glass of wine may be relaxing, but turning to the bottle to avoid wedding stress is quite obviously not a good idea.

Get regular exercise

Even if it's just a half-hour of walking a day, a well-paced amble through your neighborhood or through a scenic park is good for your heart and body, and it can also clear your mind. If you are not a regular exerciser, talk with your doctor about a good exercise plan for you, and incorporate it into your daily schedule. You may think you don't have time for a workout or a walk, but you actually don't have time *not* to. You can also consult exercise magazines for expert-created fitness routines, and reap the benefits of a regular workout.

Some brides report that they have created new partnerships with their grooms, incorporating a morning walk or workout session as shared time together doing something healthy. Or, they may spend an afternoon pursuing a shared love of sports, playing tennis, shooting hoops, or even taking some swings at the batting cages. These active outings are good bonding time, good stress relief, and good exercise.

Another part of fitness is the highly popular practice of yoga. Millions swear by the variations of this ancient practice, and studios and classes are popping up all over the place. The most highly stressed among us are urged by doctors and massage therapists to try yoga to loosen the body and release built-up stress. Yoga enthusiasts say the practice has changed their lives and given them more flexibility, more muscle strength, better posture, and more inner peace and confidence. I have taken yoga classes, and I can attest to the positive effects of this exercise form. It's a half-hour of concentration on creating healthy energy, moving the body, and clearing the mind. Research classes well if you are interested, and start at the beginner level even if you consider yourself to be a great athlete with a quick learning curve. Yoga is challenging, but the benefits are long-lasting.

The mind and stress relief

Entire books have been written about the mind-body connection and how your thoughts affect your health. You may not be worried too much about your stress levels leading to diabetes or heart disease right now. All you know is that your back is tight, your muscles are clenched, your heart is racing, and you are so stressed out by the incessant demands and details of planning your day that you feel like you're going to explode. A good workout may calm your jangled nerves, but you may need a little bit extra for your mind to slow down and for you to truly relax. No, I'm not suggesting Valium. I'm going to touch on some of the mind-healthy techniques for stress relief.

Taking a regular bath

A nightly bath can become your calm-down routine. Countless brides say their bath is their oasis, and it's where they go to escape from the demands of the day. Soaking in a warm tub (not too hot, as that raises blood pressure) that has been sprinkled with lavender bath salts or powder can melt away tension and give you some time to unwind. Books have been written about the glories of the bath as a meditation tool, and you may have already seen pictures in magazines of beautiful marble bathrooms lined with scented candles. It is truly a luxury, and it is a habit I highly recommend.

Meditation

All right, lower that eyebrow. There are lots of different kinds of meditation techniques, all suited to you particular kind of emotional needs. You may be the type who can sit in the lotus position and clear your mind as you listen to a tape of Buddhist gongs. Or you may get more use from a tape of guided relaxation exercises, as I do. You may choose walking meditation, wherein you go for a walk and consciously notice every detail and sense surrounding you.

Meditation is simply the relaxation of the mind, what I call giving it a break from the incessant inner chatter about all of the things in your life. If you can spend just 10 to 15 minutes focusing your mind on relaxing your body, you'll gain great benefits in the way of stress relief. It may not be easy at first. If you're the typical harried woman with a million things to do, it may seem like you don't have the time for this activity. But again, you don't *not* have the time. Regular mind relaxation will make you less stressed, more able to focus on decision making, less crabby, and more able to enjoy the planning process. Your partner will appreciate not being the target of your conflicted emotions, and he too may join in as you lie still on the living room floor listening to a relaxation tape. He may need it as much as you do.

I highly recommend Dr. Joan Borysenko's "Meditations for Self-Healing and Inner Power." Her soothing voice and guided relaxation exercise is the most effective stress-relief tape I've found, and I encourage you to use it for your own inner peace and adequate functioning.

Massage

We've touched on massage as part of a beauty routine, and I've already touted it as a primary method of relaxation. I can't stress enough the power and need for human touch, for muscle relaxation, and for the bonding power of massaging one another. Much has been written about the chemical releases of the body during massage, as healthy hormones emerge and toxins are freed. Beyond the science of massage, you know that it's just wonderfully relaxing and a great precursor to sex.

If you would like to incorporate massage into your routine with your partner, check out the Living Arts massage videos by massage expert Michelle Kluck. Her line includes a varied list of titles, from *Couples Massage* to *Massage for Relaxation*. You can check out her line of titles at *www.gaiam.com*.

If you're partner's not around and you need a good instant fix, try the small massage balls such as Spiky Ball, available at *www.gotyourback.com,* or reflexology textured foot rollers to ease the tension out of the bottoms of your feet.

For tension in muscles, there are all kinds of props and products, tapes and books that can guide you to a new routine of stress reduction, not just for this planning time but throughout your life together. You can establish right now the kinds of practices that will benefit you physically and emotionally, and keep you close and intimate as well.

Aromatherapy and essential oils

I must admit, I was an aromatherapy skeptic until a lavender diffuser melted my stress away during a difficult time. How, I wondered, could sniffing a scent make my life better? Well, no scent is going to erase the outside pressures of your life, but it has been proven that taking in various aromas does stimulate certain brain chemicals that lead to relaxation. In fact, some scents do far more than that, acting as analgesics and other healing properties.

I don't know about the idea of aromatherapy and the use of essential oils as instant cures, but I do know that filling a room or a home with a pleasing scent does have relaxating effects. The room smells wonderful, and your shoulders come down from up around your ears as you take in the pleasing scents. It's the same idea as the way you feel when you've just baked fresh bread. That amazing, warm smell instantly relaxes you. The smell of green apples, studies say, is also a relaxant.

Much has been written about aromatherapy, and entire new lines of scented products are extremely popular now. As interest in this area of relaxation is higher now, more information is available on the benefits and uses of each scent. I've listed for you a small sampling of the most popular aromatherapy oils, plus a brief description of their effects, and I've starred the ones that are said to be aphrodisiacs. I'll leave the testing of those theories up to you, and I encourage you to follow usage directions on any aromatherapy product exactly as written.

Basil*:	Helps ability to concentrate.
Bergamot:	Fights anxiety and depression.
Chamomile:	Calms.
Cinnamon*:	Fights fatigue and depression.
Clary Sage:	Stress-reducer, fights anxiety and depression.
Frankincense*:	Calming and meditation
Geranium:	Relaxes.
Jasmine*:	Fights depression, tension.
Lavender:	Calms, helps you sleep, relaxes.
Lemon:	Refreshes, boosts energy.
Marjoram:	Mild sedative, helps fight insomnia.
Neroli*:	Fights nervous tension and insomnia.
Patchouli*:	Relaxes, calms anxiety.
Peppermint:	Calms, aids digestion, relaxes muscles.
Rose*:	Balances, fights stress, anxiety, and sadness.
Rosemary:	Uplifts and energizes.
Sage:	Relaxes.
Sandalwood:	Relaxes.
Ylang Ylang*:	Fights stress, anger, and frustration.

Of course, there are many, many more versions of essential oils and aromatherapy products out there. Stores such as Forevergreen in Hoboken, New Jersey create aromatherapy massage oils, soaps, creams, and lotions with various herbs to create the right formula for you. Michelle Weintraub, owner of Forevergreen and creator of many of the custom made products there, invites clients to try samples of the most aromatic, relaxing products. Check out her line at *www.thesoaphut.com* or look for other aromatherapy products, such as the Healing Garden line, carried at many locations.

Alternative medicine

If exploring the stress-busting avenues out there right now is interesting to you, you will run across classes and demonstrations for many New Age practices, such as tai chi, chi gong, acupuncture, Bach Flower Essence, reiki, energy repatterning, and the like. I cannot speak for or against the validity, effects, practices, or recommendations of any of these offerings. All I can do is urge you to do some research on them, ask friends who have experience, and consider strongly whether this avenue is right for you. Various magazines and New Age Web sites can give you the information you need.

Sex—the ultimate stress relief

Don't forget that intimacy with your partner is always going to be the most relaxing, boding experience you can have. Not just the actual lovemaking, but the romantic build-up, the foreplay, and the after-cuddling, the laughing and touching and talking. In bed, you're a couple in love, unconcerned with all of the little details of the wedding itself. In bed, you're sharing your love in a physical and emotional way, strengthening the bond between you.

Sometimes you just need to get away

If the wedding process is truly stressful, with outside interference, difficult family dynamics, and a limiting budget, all of the lavender and great sex in the world is not going to bring you the escape and relaxation you need. In these cases, it's time to just get away.

Stress meltdown aside, it's always a good idea to have a life outside of the wedding planning. Too many couples spend an entire year having the wedding as the center of their world, and they simply don't do anything else. It's important to be yourself, and to be the couple that you are, rather than the planning bride and the planning couple. If you have kids, they too need to know that they have your attention, and that you are still their parents.

That said, here is a list of fun escapes from the world of weddings, where you can relax, have fun, and be yourselves:

- Go to a sporting event.
- Go to a cultural event.
- Go to a ski resort or country club for some activity.
- Go camping.
- Go for a weekend away at a bed-and-breakfast.
- Spend the day in a quaint, touristy village, shopping at antiques stores and seeing the sights.
- Go to flea markets.
- Spend a day at the beach or a lake.
- Go for a dinner cruise or fishing trip.
- Visit museums or art galleries.
- Go dancing.
- Try new restaurants.
- Take an adult-education course together, such as French cooking classes, wine appreciation, watercolors, or photography.
- Go on a picnic, just the two of you, in an apple grove or scenic park.
- Go to an arcade or similar fun-oriented club, like Dave and Buster's, and just play for hours.
- See great movies.
- Go to local special events, such as readings by visiting authors.
- Go to nearby town festivals.

Your town newspaper is likely filled with fun things to do, and there's always an activity at the local bookstore. Even if your schedule is jam-packed with work, with planning the wedding, and with caring for your kids, make sure you spend time doing something that's just fun and not rife with details or problems. You'll find that you're all more relaxed and the wedding planning process is much easier. Best of all, you're setting great new routines for an enjoyable life together in the future.

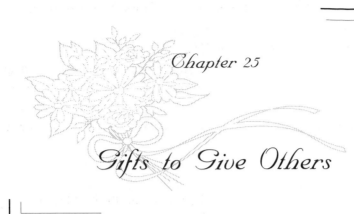

Chapter 25

Gifts to Give Others

One of the best parts of a wedding is the giving and receiving of love. Although you will of course express your love through hugs and kisses, smiles, and kind words, you'll also express your deepest feelings of gratitude and affection through the giving of gifts. From your bridal party to your parents to your kids to each other, you'll compile a gift list that shows how much all of these people mean to you. One of the fun jobs during the wedding planning is finding the right presents for the right people, knowing you're giving them something meaningful, something they will not only use, but also remember you by.

Gifts for the bridal party

It goes without saying that the bride and groom traditionally give gifts to their wedding attendants as a way of thanking them for their help and their role in the wedding. Although the first-time bride usually gets the same item for all of her maids, you may choose to get different presents (in the same price range) for each of your attendants. Second-time brides have more varied attendants; they're not all 22-year-old college roommates. Some may be teenagers, some may be colleagues, and some may be older women who are special to them. With a mixed bridal party, you will find it much easier to buy individualized gifts rather than find one thing that is suitable for everyone. Your options open up, and the shopping spree is much more enjoyable.

Here, then, are some ideas for all of the members of your bridal party:

Maid of honor and bridesmaids:

Jewelry.

Jewelry boxes.

Wine glass sets.

Wine cooler in silver plate, monogrammed.

Wine basket.

Silver picture frame.

Art deco picture frame.

Music box.

Godiva chocolates.

Broadway play tickets or other special event tickets.

Gift certificates for a day at a spa.

Subscription to favorite magazines.

Day planner for the next year.

Maid service or organizer service for one year.

Dried flower bouquet or decorative swag.

Personalized photo albums.

Perfume.

Crystal ornaments (for a holiday wedding).

The best man, ushers, and groomsmen

Silver money clips.

Personalized golf balls.

Golf accessories (gloves, tees, club covers, etc.).

Day planners.

Crystal beer mug with silver name plate.

Wine and wine rack.

Wine cooler, monogrammed.

Tickets to a ball game or an event.

Cigars and cigar accessories.

Sterling silver key rings.

Cufflinks.

Shaving kits.

Child attendants in the bridal party

Children's jewelry.

Jewelry box.

Music box.

The hot toy of the moment.

Gift certificate to a toy store.

Name plaque for their bedrooms.

Stuffed animals.

Hand-held computer game (just state that they can't play with it on the day of the wedding).

Educational CD-ROMs.

For family and visitors

Parents

Gift certificates to favorite
gourmet restaurants.
Bottle of Dom Perignon or Cristal.
Gift certificate to a day spa.
Wine basket.
Wines and wine rack.
Wine cooler, monogrammed.

Music box.
Silver frame.
Godiva chocolates.
Flowers or plants.
Crystal or china vase.
Tiffany & Co. key chain.

Out-of-town visitors staying in a hotel

Snack basket containing sodas,
bottled water, juices, crackers,
small liquor bottles, cookies,
and fruit.
Gift certificate for hotel breakfast.
Gift certificate for day spa or
hotel's spa services.
Gift certificate for a professional
massage through the hotel spa.

Disposable cameras.
Godiva chocolates.
Bottle of wine or champagne.
Fruit and cheese platter delivered
to the room after hours.
Kids' basket containing children's
activity books, coloring books,
small toys, juice boxes, candies,
and cookies.

For children of the marriage, any age:

Family medallion.
Heirloom jewelry.
Gift certificates for their favorite
stores.
Their own phone line (they've
been asking forever).

A raise in their allowance (it's
about time).
Event tickets.
Computer games or educational
CD-ROMs.
Lessons in a chosen activity (dance,
horseback riding, sports, etc.).

For the bride and groom gift exchange

As thrilling as all your gifts will be to your loved ones and guests, none will be as memorable as those you exchange with each other. A lot of thought and sentimentality goes into making these choices, and it is something you will remember forever, so consider the list of suggestions below, think of what more personalized items you can get each other, and choose an item that truly speaks of your devotion to one another.

For the groom

A framed picture of the two of you.

A year of golf lessons.

A new set of golf clubs.

A motorcycle driving course.

Lessons in his chosen hobby.

A great jacket that he's been wanting forever.

An inscribed watch.

A cigar humidor with supply of cigars.

A case of vintage wines and champagnes for his collection.

New office furniture.

A professional nameplate for his desk.

A new pet, such as the pedigreed Alaskan husky puppy he's always wanted.

A portable laptop computer.

For the bride

Gift certificates.

Silver jewelry.

Pearl jewelry.

Jewelry with her birthstone.

A day or week at a spa.

Tuition to a class she's been wanting to take.

A week at a bed-and-breakfast as a separate trip from your honeymoon.

A portable laptop computer.

A nameplate for her office.

New office furniture.

A new pet, such as that pedigreed cocker spaniel she's always wanted.

The services of a personal organizer or maid for one year.

Shared couple gifts

Instead of getting separate gifts, you might decide to join forces (and bank accounts) for a more expensive shared gift:

Paying off college loans.

A new car.

A new house.

Remodeling of old house.

New landscaping.

Installation of a garden.

Installation of a pool.

A stock portfolio.

A new home computer.

New furniture.

A new entertainment center.

Paying off old bills (not romantic, but worth the peace of mind).

Home gourmet delivery service for a year (if you're both too busy to cook).

A professionally edited videotape of your history together.

Again, this is just a jumping-off point, a list to get you thinking. Because this category of gift should be the most personalized, according to what your mate truly loves and would appreciate, take time to make your selection. Check out other sources. You know your partner well, so think about what would bring out the most deeply felt emotion. It could be a rare collector's item such as a first edition of a favorite book, a signed autograph from a favorite actor, a night at the theater watching a favorite comedian, or even a homemade book of redeemable X-rated "coupons." The choice is up to you. I know you'll choose well.

Chapter 26

The 24-Hour Countdown

The day before the wedding

The big day is almost here, and by the time 24 hours pass, you'll be married to your best friend. But today is today, and there is probably a long list of things to do before you get to tomorrow. It's important to be organized, to leave nothing to memory, and to write down everything that needs to be done.

If you've followed all the advice in this book, your major tasks are all behind you, and it's just the last-minute things that need to be done. Others may be able to help, so share the load and keep yourself from getting exhausted today.

The day before the wedding, for most brides, is filled with making confirmation calls, picking up out-of-town relatives, and taking care of all the little things that by nature cannot be done until the last minute. It may mean cooking, baking, picking up orders, decorating, or setting up rental items. It might be observing the workers putting up the tent, or it might be relaxing with friends and getting ready for the rehearsal later in the day.

No matter what is on your to-do list, keep yourself balanced and organized, efficient and stress-free. Whatever arises can be handled either through replacement or improvisation. Stay focused, allow others to step in and help, and remember to enjoy the moments.

Delegating

You read earlier about the benefits of delegating some of the smaller jobs and accepting others' offers to help. For your last-minute tasks, you may need to rely on more help than you anticipated. Several little things may pop up that still have to be covered. Some new issues may arise, and you may need some help with handling the details that will make your day run more smoothly.

The day of the wedding

On the morning of the wedding, all may seem rushed and harried, as you attend to your last-minute things to do, plus those of everyone else. Countless brides have spoken of frantic car rides to the store to buy small white candles for the centerpieces, new contact lenses, and even a replacement wedding cake when it became evident that the hired baker was not going to come through.

Unfortunately, last-minute snafus do happen. You should expect them, and you should have a backup plan. I would advise assigning someone now to be your wedding-day rescue person, the person who is not in the bridal party who will be your savior when it comes time to run to the store for a new pair of pantyhose. It may be your wedding coordinator who does this, or it may be your close friend and neighbor. Regardless of the title, you must have someone you know you can count on no matter what situations arise on the morning of the wedding.

Because every wedding is different, I cannot advise you specifically about what needs to be done before the official action starts, but I can supply a general list of details to take care of on the morning of the wedding:

- Eat breakfast, even if you're not having a bridal brunch. Be well-fueled.
- Be sure you have all of your wedding accessories laid out and ready to go.
- Be sure you have an extra pair of pantyhose in case you snag the first one.
- Have your maids join you at the bridal salon for your makeovers.
- Get instructions on touching up your makeup during the day.
- Call to confirm delivery of the flowers and cake.
- Call to confirm the arrival of the limos.

- Be sure you have the marriage license in hand.
- Be sure you have the rings.
- Be sure you have all of the fee and tipping envelopes for the vendors filled, marked, sealed, and brought with you to the wedding.
- Be sure you have your garter on.
- Be sure there is a plan for you to get your honeymoon luggage to the hotel room after the reception.
- Be sure your plane tickets are in your carry-on bag.
- Be sure your purse, wallet, identification, credit cards, and house keys are packed in your carry-on as well.
- Be sure there is a plan for your wedding gifts to be brought back to your home after the reception.
- Be sure there is a plan for the top layer of your cake to be saved, wrapped, and delivered back to your home, if you so desire.
- Check the weather forecast for the day, to see if you'll need to bring umbrellas for later on.
- Be sure you have your emergency bag.
- Be sure you have your copy of your vows.
- Be sure you have any inhalers, medications, or insulin you might need during the day.
- Share some quiet moments with your family before things get really busy.

For the marrying mom

The wedding morning is not going to be your circus alone. Your children will also have their breakdowns, their last-minute needs, and a host of swirling emotions as the wedding day takes shape before their eyes. Again, remember that this is an emotional time for all of you. Your kids may need the assurance of spending a little time alone with you before all of the dressing and picture-taking begins.

A good way to make sure the kids are not overloaded with stress is to make them an important focus of the day as well. Bring them to the salon for their makeovers, tell them they look great, and assure them gently that they'll do a good job during the wedding. You know your child best. You know her style, and you know how to handle her serious moments. She may not be the type to talk it out. She may just want to hang out in her room and avoid all the fuss. Just allow her her space, and do not push her to enjoy the moment the way you would want her to. Seek peace here, and don't add to any stress.

Your kids have a checklist of their own as they prepare themselves for the wedding:

- Be sure their outfits are laid out, along with all of their accessories.
- Take them to the salon for their makeovers.
- Be sure they eat breakfast or are part of the bridal brunch. Include foods they like in the menu.
- Allow them to interview you on home videotape. Kids love to be a part of big events, and this may be a creative way for them to participate.
- Be sure they are dressed in time for the photos. Ideally, you should help dress them first and then dress yourself.
- Be sure kids have a copy of their ceremony speeches with them.
- Be sure they are wearing the family medallion or jewelry gift you gave them last night. (Don't nag, though. Your child may not be ready to wear the family medallion. Although it's a strong symbol for you, your child may need some time to warm up to it. Just encourage gently, and be prepared to hear no—gracefully—from them.)
- Be sure plans are set with whoever will be watching them while you are away.
- If they will be coming on a family honeymoon, be sure their bags are packed, including their ID, passport, and any important items such as medication, inhalers, sporting equipment, and so on. Also, be sure there is a plan to get their luggage delivered to their hotel room after the reception.
- Spend quiet time with them before the action starts.
- Take fun, candid photos of you and the kids before the official photos take place.

And, you're off!

Before you know it, the time will come when you're ready to be whisked away in your limousine or classic car. Your entourage is at the ready, and you attract plenty of attention as you wheel through your neighborhood on your way to the wedding. Enjoy every moment. Savor the meaning of this final journey from your home as a single woman. Know that in just a few short minutes, you will be joined forever to your true love. You're about to start a new family, blend a new family, combine your lives into something new and exciting. You've planned this day for a long time, and I have no doubt that you've created the wedding of your dreams. It may be flawless, it may not be. But there is something to be said for less-than-perfect weddings:

> "All we needed at our reception were locusts, and then the whole apocalypse theme would have been complete. We had rain, mud, wind, no lights, our cake melted off the table, and my ex showed up drunk and had to be removed. I was just stunned, but I learned a lot in the way my husband and I handled each crisis. It may have been a disappointment to have these things happen on our wedding day, but we look at the up side. At least we know that we work well together as a team, not even the forces of nature can keep us apart, and my new husband is a man of class in how he asked my ex to respect my happiness and remove himself from where he was not welcome. So from a potentially bad situation, I received a powerful message: my new husband fights for my honor, and he loves me more than I ever thought before. If I had any jitters, they're gone now."
>
> —Jane

So whatever happens that you didn't expect or didn't plan, look for the bright side and for the positive message. And know that after all of the parts of the wedding—the elements you've planned so carefully—are done, you will be married. That is what it's all about.

Now, good luck to you!
I wish you all the love, joy, and happiness
in the world,
in your marriage,
and in your new life.

Afterword

Planning a New Life Together

Too many second-time brides get so caught up in the planning of the wedding that they forget to look at the bigger picture. They forget about the issues and challenges that real life, outside of the one-day event of the wedding, is going to hand them, and they do not take the appropriate steps to ensure a successful marriage. They forget that not only are they planning a wedding, but they are also planning to share their lives with their partner, and perhaps to combine two families into one.

I cannot address all of the myriad details that go into making an encore marriage work, but I can offer these precious pieces of advice from family therapist Paula Bortnichak, Ph.D.:

1. Before you can begin a new life together, you must make sure that both of you have worked out the issues from your first marriages completely. All of the underlying fears and anger issues have to be dealt with so that you can work through them, learn from them, and accept them. A complete inspection of your inner issues as related to your first marriage will prevent you from repeating the same patterns and mistakes in this marriage.

2. Look closely at what made your first marriage successful and what made it unsuccessful. Nothing is black and white; nothing is all good or all bad. Acknowledge that there were some good times, you did love each other, and you both had a part in the ending of the marriage. Examine what your part was, whether you were impatient, had poor communication skills, or were not completely honest with your partner. This is a

difficult task, as it often brings up feelings of guilt or anger, but you must work through them in advance of this new marriage in order to know your own strengths and weaknesses. Only then can you forgive yourself, accept your past, and look forward to the future.

3. Acknowledge who you are today. Know your personality and your priorities, your habits and patterns. To be in a healthy relationship is to know who you are, and to stay who you are. It is the mark of a poor relationship when one or both members allow themselves to change to suit a partner's habits and patterns. Such unspoken melding causes one or both people to lose themselves, which fosters resentment, and that in turn leads to the end of a marriage. Know yourself, keep yourself, and stay true to yourself at the core. Yes, there is room for small changes and cooperation, but you should never change who you are to keep a relationship.

4. Know what's important to you in this relationship. It may be your communication, the fun you have, the support you give and get. Always keep those values at the forefront as your relationship moves through time.

5. Remember that nothing ever stays the same. You will experience change in life, and you must learn how to work together to adjust to constantly shifting situations and experiences. This is one of the biggest lessons of life. You must get used to it and remember to be flexible while staying true to yourself and your partnership.

6. Keep your independence. Continue to enjoy your own individual activities and interests, and allow your partner to have his. Doing everything together is a sign of an insecure, young relationship, so allow yourselves some space and freedom, and retain the same personalities you've enjoyed in one another since you met.

7. Know your partner completely. You may have learned the hard way the first time around that it's more important to know who your partner is inside than to know where your Saturday night dates are going to be. An immature relationship that does not last is one in which the partners hide facets of themselves, or do not venture into deep topics. A fear of intimacy leads couples to avoid discussing the big topics, ones that might change how they feel about each other. In your serious relationship, you should feel free to discuss where you agree and where you differ on the subjects of religion, politics, education, the arts,

current events, and so on. With more self-knowledge (which comes with age), you have more depth and can share more of who you are. You're also a better judge of character.

8. Know the status of both of your past relationships. Especially if you both have children, and you both have contact with your exes, be sure there is not remaining hostility related to that history. Even if it takes short-term therapy, be sure that both you and your partner are not enacting with each other issues that are related to your previous marriages. You both must have peace with your exes, in-laws who see the children, and mutual friends.

9. Allow your partner to have contact with the old part of his life, such as you might want with yours. He may have reached a cease-fire with his ex-wife, and they may be on friendly terms. It will only cause harm to your relationship if you seethe with jealousy over his connection to his ex-wife. They have children together. They must have contact with one another. You can't tell him to cut all ties. So deal with your own fear and insecurity, and make peace with his connections and ability to rise above holding a grudge for the sake of the kids.

10. Handle the money issue. Nothing causes more fights in new marriages than differing money styles. Discuss in a mature, rational way your shared views on maintaining separate accounts, opening a joint account in addition to your separate accounts, and other monetary issues. Communicate well on this factor so that there are no unspoken resentments. The "what's mine is yours" school is not entirely applicable anymore, so discuss your views and expectations together completely before you get married.

11. Handle the responsibility issue. Know who's going to manage the housework, the kids' schedules, the parent-teacher meetings, the drop-offs at events and custody trades. Treat all tasks as your equal responsibility, and stay far away from the topic of what's a woman's task and what's a man's task. Divide responsibilities amongst yourselves and the kids, and create a household that works well together as a supportive team.

12. Handle the sex issue. No doubt you know what each other's preferences are, and if you've lived together you know each other's patterns and favorite times of day for lovemaking. Understand that when there are other problems in a relationship, they very often are expressed through a couple's sex life, or lack thereof. So if there is a problem with your sex life, find the hidden issue or problem, and work it out.

Helping the children to adjust

Dr. Bortnichak also provides some tips for helping your children to adjust to the blending of your families. These tips may enable you to understand what your child might be feeling, and you should use them to help facilitate open conversations with your kids.

- There will be insecurity among the kids from both sides. Children like order, and they do not like change. This blending of your families throws their world into chaos, and they will need you to understand the fact that they are afraid of what their new life will be like.

- Their birth order changes. Your oldest son may not be the oldest child in the family anymore. Now he has a big brother who gets privileges before he does. It may be a shock to him to see you handing your car keys to "the new brother." Understand that where kids rank in the family is important to them, so the shuffling of position is likely to ruffle some feathers. You can remedy this potential problem by treating all children as equals, allowing all the basic respect and open communication paths they deserve. Set clear, written rules about which privileges come at which age, such as when dating and driving are allowed, and have all children adhere to those rules.

- Allow the children access to their other parents, if the relationship is comfortable and safe for them. Do not restrict their access to their father, thinking that it would confuse their bonding time with their new dad. This tactic works in the opposite direction and is certain to fail.

- Pay attention to the kids. Don't get so caught up in being newlyweds that your roles as parents come second. Although you should enjoy some time alone, the kids are going to need your attention now more than ever. So plan group and individual activities with your kids.

- Hold family meetings, where all members of the family are free to discuss their problems or concerns. Good communication requires the absence of assumptions, and kids may need a few meetings in order to get their needs met.

- Kids are more savvy about blended families now. They've seen plenty of examples of it on television and in movies, and many of their school friends may be from combined homes. Yet just because they're savvy about the topic doesn't mean they are handling their individual feelings well. Although they may have friends to talk to, they are then at risk of feeling weird if their experience doesn't match their friends' blasé attitudes. So you should be the one they come to for counsel, or you can take your child to a qualified family therapist. Don't let another 13-year-old control your child's thoughts and self-esteem.

❧ Don't try to be the best friend, or to buy the kids' affection. Kids are smart. They see right through what you're doing and will in fact respect you less. They'll learn exactly which strings to pull to get what they want from you, and they know how to push the guilt and fear button with you. You can be friendly, but you are not your children's peer.

❧ Remember that, depending upon their ages, your kids may be experiencing any number of inner traumas. Growing up is hard, and they're facing peer pressure, self-esteem issues, and perhaps their own relationship issues. There's a lot going on in your child's life besides your marriage, and if you assume that your child's bad mood is all about you, you will further close the doors of communication with your child. If your child is not adjusting well to the change, is losing or gaining weight, has sleep problems, big mood swings, or a drop in grades, talk to a qualified therapist about the signs of adjustment disorders, depression, or addictions. Don't panic. But don't blind yourself to your child's struggles.

You will find many books on the subject of merging two families into one. Do your own reading, engage in therapy to help you make the adjustments and deal with any underlying issues or fears, and begin your new married life on the best foundation possible. Only with commitment and dedication will your marriage last a lifetime. It's not about getting married. It's about being married. It's not about the cake. It's about the sweetness of your life together.

I wish you all the luck in the world, and I hope you will have a wonderful future together!

Appendix A

Master Contact List

For the utmost in organization, fill these pages out completely and make several copies of each for distribution when necessary. This way, if you need to delegate a task to a helpful attendant, she already has the phone numbers and e-mail addresses at hand. The bridal party can stay in contact with one another (to talk about your gift, perhaps!) and everyone will know where the salons and shops are.

Bride: _____

Address: _____

Phone number: _____ Work number:_____

Cell phone:_____ Fax: _____

E-mail: _____

Groom:_____

Address: _____

Phone number: _____ Work number:_____

Cell phone:_____ Fax: _____

E-mail: _____

Maid of Honor: _____

Address: _____

Phone number: _____ Work number:_____

Cell phone:_____ Fax: _____

E-mail: _____

Bridesmaid: _____

Address: _____

Phone number: _____ Work number:_____

Cell phone:_____ Fax: _____

E-mail: _____

Bridesmaid: _____

Address: _____

Phone number: _____ Work number:_____

Cell phone:_____ Fax: _____

E-mail: _____

Bridesmaid: _____

Address: _____

Phone number: _____ Work number:_____

Cell phone:_____ Fax: _____

E-mail: _____

Bridesmaid: _____

Address: _____

Phone number: _____ Work number:_____

Cell phone:_____ Fax: _____

E-mail: _____

Flower girl's parents: _____

Address: _____

Phone number: _____ Work number:_____

Cell phone:_____ Fax: _____

E-mail: _____

Flower girl's parents: _____

Address: _____

Phone number: _____ Work number:_____

Cell phone:_____ Fax: _____

E-mail: _____

Best Man: _____

Address: _____

Phone number: _____   Work number: _____

Cell phone: _____   Fax: _____

E-mail: _____

Usher/Groomsman: _____

Address: _____

Phone number: _____   Work number: _____

Cell phone: _____   Fax: _____

E-mail: _____

Usher/Groomsman: _____

Address: _____

Phone number: _____   Work number: _____

Cell phone: _____   Fax: _____

E-mail: _____

Usher/Groomsman: _____

Address: _____

Phone number: _____   Work number: _____

Cell phone: _____   Fax: _____

E-mail: _____

Usher/Groomsman: _____

Address: _____

Phone number: _____   Work number: _____

Cell phone: _____   Fax: _____

E-mail: _____

Ring -bearer's parents: _____

Address: _____

Phone number: _____   Work number: _____

Cell phone: _____   Fax: _____

E-mail: _____

Parents of the bride: _____

Address: _____

Phone number: _____ Work number: _____

Cell phone: _____ Fax: _____

E-mail: _____

Parents of the groom: _____

Address: _____

Phone number: _____ Work number: _____

Cell phone: _____ Fax: _____

E-mail: _____

Officiant: _____

Address: _____

Phone number: _____ Work number: _____

Cell phone: _____ Fax: _____

E-mail: _____

Wedding coordinator: _____

Address: _____

Phone number: _____ Work number: _____

Cell phone: _____ Fax: _____

E-mail: _____

Bridal gown shop manager: _____

Address: _____

Phone number: _____ Work number: _____

Cell phone: _____ Fax: _____

E-mail: _____

Bridesmaids' gowns shop manager: _____

Address: _____

Phone number: _____ Work number: _____

Cell phone: _____ Fax: _____

E-mail: _____

Seamstress: _____

Address: _____

Phone number: _____ Work number: _____

Cell phone: _____ Fax: _____

E-mail: _____

Tuxedo shop manager: _____

Address: _____

Phone number: _____ Work number: _____

Cell phone: _____ Fax: _____

E-mail: _____

Shoe Store: _____

Address: _____

Phone number: _____ Work number: _____

Cell phone: _____ Fax: _____

E-mail: _____

Musicians: _____

Address: _____

Phone number: _____ Work number: _____

Cell phone: _____ Fax: _____

E-mail: _____

Floral designer: _____

Address: _____

Phone number: _____ Work number: _____

Cell phone: _____ Fax: _____

E-mail: _____

Invitations salesperson: _____

Address: _____

Phone number: _____ Work number: _____

Cell phone: _____ Fax: _____

E-mail: _____

Calligrapher: _____

Address: _____

Phone number: _____ Work number: _____

Cell phone: _____ Fax: _____

E-mail: _____

Caterer: _____

Address: _____

Phone number: _____ Work number: _____

Cell phone: _____ Fax: _____

E-mail: _____

Cake baker: _____

Address: _____

Phone number: _____ Work number: _____

Cell phone: _____ Fax: _____

E-mail: _____

Reception hall manager: _____

Address: _____

Phone number: _____ Work number: _____

Cell phone: _____ Fax: _____

E-mail: _____

Photographer: _____

Address: _____

Phone number: _____ Work number: _____

Cell phone: _____ Fax: _____

E-mail: _____

Videographer: _____

Address: _____

Phone number: _____ Work number: _____

Cell phone: _____ Fax: _____

E-mail: _____

Limousine/transportation company: _____

Address: _____

Phone number: _____   Work number: _____

Cell phone: _____   Fax: _____

E-mail: _____

Hotel manager: _____

Address: _____

Phone number: _____   Work number: _____

Cell phone: _____   Fax: _____

E-mail: _____

Reception entertainment: _____

Address: _____

Phone number: _____   Work number: _____

Cell phone: _____   Fax: _____

E-mail: _____

Travel agent: _____

Address: _____

Phone number: _____   Work number: _____

Cell phone: _____   Fax: _____

E-mail: _____

Rental agent: _____

Address: _____

Phone number: _____   Work number: _____

Cell phone: _____   Fax: _____

E-mail: _____

Beauty salon: _____

Address: _____

Phone number: _____   Work number: _____

Cell phone: _____   Fax: _____

E-mail: _____

Registry specialist: _____

Address: _____

Phone number: _____ Work number: _____

Cell phone: _____ Fax: _____

E-mail: _____

Attorney *(name change, divorce related paperwork)*: _____

Address: _____

Phone number: _____ Work number: _____

Cell phone: _____ Fax: _____

E-mail: _____

Family counselor: _____

Address: _____

Phone number: _____ Work number: _____

Cell phone: _____ Fax: _____

E-mail: _____

Other: _____

Address: _____

Phone number: _____ Work number: _____

Cell phone: _____ Fax: _____

E-mail: _____

Other: _____

Address: _____

Phone number: _____ Work number: _____

Cell phone: _____ Fax: _____

E-mail: _____

Other: _____

Address: _____

Phone number: _____ Work number: _____

Cell phone: _____ Fax: _____

E-mail: _____

Appendix B

Master Guest List

Name of Guest	Invitation Sent?	Attending?	Gift Received?	Thank You Sent?

Name of Guest	Invitation Sent?	Attending?	Gift Received?	Thank You Sent?

Appendix C

Seating Chart

During Ceremony:

1st Row Left:

_____

_____

_____

_____

_____

_____

2nd Row Left:

_____

_____

_____

_____

_____

3rd Row Left:

_____

_____

_____

_____

_____

1st Row Right:

_____

_____

_____

_____

_____

_____

2nd Row Right:

_____

_____

_____

_____

_____

3rd Row Right:

_____

_____

_____

_____

_____

During Reception:

Table number or name: _____

Guests:

_____   _____

_____   _____

_____   _____

_____   _____

_____   _____

Table number or name: _____

Guests:

_____   _____

_____   _____

_____   _____

_____   _____

_____   _____

Table number or name: _____

Guests:

_____   _____

_____   _____

_____   _____

_____   _____

_____   _____

Table number or name: _____

Guests:

_____   _____

_____   _____

_____   _____

_____   _____

_____   _____

Table number or name: _____
Guests:

_____   _____

_____   _____

_____   _____

_____   _____

_____   _____

Table number or name: _____
Guests:

_____   _____

_____   _____

_____   _____

_____   _____

_____   _____

Table number or name: _____
Guests:

_____   _____

_____   _____

_____   _____

_____   _____

_____   _____

Table number or name: _____
Guests:

_____   _____

_____   _____

_____   _____

_____   _____

_____   _____

Appendix D

Who Pays for What

Item	Who Pays	Budgeted Amount	Actual Amount
Engagement dinner			
Invitations			
Invitation postage			
Wedding announcements			
Programs			
Place cards			
Maps			
Invitation packet materials			
Calligraphy			
Copying expenses			
Thank-you notes			
Guest book and pen			
Wedding stationery			
Bride's gown			
Bride's shoes			
Bride's accessories			
Bride's makeup			
Bride's hair			
Veil or headpiece			
Undergarments			
Jewelry			

Item	Who Pays	Budgeted Amount	Actual Amount
Groom's tuxedo or suit			
Groom's Shoes			
Groom's accessories			
Bridesmaids' Attire (opt)			
Child attendants' attire (opt)			
Wedding consultant			
Wedding consultant's assistants			
Wedding planner			
Wedding journal			
Bride's bouquet			
Bridesmaids' bouquets			
Maid/Matron of Honor's Bouquet			
Boutonnieres			
Corsages			
Child attendants' flowers			
Centerpieces			
Room décor			
Altar décor			
Site décor			
Memorial wreaths			
Unity candle			
Candles			
Aisle runner			
Chuppah			
Ring pillow			

Item	Who Pays	Budgeted Amount	Actual Amount
Photography package			
Extra photos			
Wedding albums			
Wedding video			
Video copies			
Video cases			
Limousine service			
Extra transportation			
Ceremony site fee			
Permits			
Officiant's fee			
Musicians' fee			
Marriage license			
Bloodwork fees			
Legal fees			
Counseling fees			
Rehearsal fees			
Rehearsal dinner			
Travel for guests			
Lodging for guests			
Reception site fee			
Caterer			
Cake and dessert			
Liquor			
Garter			
Cake knife			
Cake server			
Toasting flutes			

Item	Who Pays	Budgeted Amount	Actual Amount
Rentals			
Entertainment			
Parking/Valet			
Tips			
Favors			
Throwaway cameras			
Décor			
Gifts for parents			
Gifts for bridal party			
Bride's Gift			
Groom's gift			
Gifts to children			
Gifts to special attendants			
Wedding night lodging			
Honeymoon			
Transportation to/from airport			
Car rentals			
Bride's trousseau			
Groom's honeymoon wardrobe			
Honeymoon packing needs			
House-sitter			
Pet-sitter			
Long-distance phone			
Souvenirs			
Name change process (opt.)			
Name changes for kids (opt.)			
Moving expenses			
Thank-you note postage			

Appendix E

Location Comparison Sheets

Name of site: _____

Address: _____

Phone: _____

Contact name: _____

Capacity: _____

Licensed? _____

Insured: _____

Number of events at same time: _____

Parking: _____

Valet: _____

Restrooms OK? _____

Complete service package (linens, tables, chairs, bar, etc?) _____

Bartender/caterer/baker included? _____

Contract specifications: _____

Signed contract received: _____

Notes on beauty of the site: _____

_____

_____

Further notes: _____

_____

_____

_____

_____

_____

Name of site: _____

Address: _____

Phone: _____

Contact name: _____

Capacity: _____

Licensed? _____

Insured: _____

Number of events at same time: _____

Parking: _____

Valet: _____

Restrooms OK? _____

Complete service package (linens, tables, chairs, bar, etc?) _____

Bartender/caterer/baker included? _____

Contract specifications: _____

Signed contract received: _____

Notes on beauty of the site: _____

_____

_____

Further notes: _____

_____

_____

_____

_____

_____

_____

_____

_____

_____

_____

Appendix F

Bridesmaids' Gown
Information Sheet

Gown store: _____

Address: _____

Phone number: _____

Hours: _____

Contact name: _____

Gown style number: _____

Designer: _____

Size ordered: _____

Deposit amount: _____

Date deposit left: _____

Free alterations? _____

Delivery date: _____

Final payment due: _____

Contract specific and signed? _____

Fittings scheduled? _____

Shoes ordered: _____

Accessories ordered: _____

Final payment made: _____

Appendix G

Wedding Gown Information Sheet

Gown store: _____

Address: _____

Phone number: _____

Hours: _____

Contact name: _____

Gown Style number: _____

Designer: _____

Size ordered: _____

Deposit amount: _____

Date deposit left: _____

Free alterations? _____

Delivery date: _____

Final payment due: _____

Contract specific and signed? _____

Veil ordered: _____

Location: _____

Phone number: _____

Price and payment made: _____

Shoes ordered: _____

Accessories ordered: _____

Appendix H

Tuxedo Information Sheet

Tuxedo store: _____

Address: _____

Phone: _____

Hours: _____

Contact name: _____

Tuxedo style number: _____

Designer: _____

Size ordered: _____

Deposit amount: _____

Date deposit left: _____

Free alterations? _____

Pickup date: _____

Final payment due: _____

Contract specific and signed? _____

Fittings scheduled? _____

Shoes ordered: _____

Accessories ordered: _____

Final payment made: _____

Appendix I

Wedding Order Details Sheet

Rings:

Style: _____

Sizes: _____

Fitting: _____

Engraving: _____

Price: _____

Contract signed: _____

Delivery date: _____

Appraisal: _____

Insurance: _____

Invitations:

Style: _____

Catalog name: _____

Store name: _____

Contact name: _____

Number ordered: _____

Envelopes and extras ordered: _____

Contract signed: _____

Deposit made: _____

Delivery date: _____

Final payment: _____

Limousines:

Company: _____

Contact name: _____

Type of cars: _____

Number of cars: _____

Color of cars: _____

Directions given: _____

Extras included in package: _____

Deposit made: _____

Contract signed: _____

Final payment due: _____

Caterer:

Name: _____

Company: _____

Tastings: _____

Menu chosen: _____

Package price: _____

Setup and clean-up: _____

Contract signed: _____

Deposit made: _____

Final payment due: _____

Photographer:

Name: _____

Company name: _____

Package price: _____

Extras: _____

Contract signed: _____

Deposit paid: _____

Directions given: _____

When pictures will be available: _____

Final payment due: _____

Videographer:

Name:_____

Company name: _____

Package price: _____

Extras: _____

Contract signed: _____

Deposit paid: _____

Directions given:_____

When pictures will be available: _____

Final payment due: _____

Cake Baker:

Name:_____

Company: _____

Design of cake: _____

Price: _____

Delivery fee: _____

Deposit made:_____

Contract signed: _____

Final payment due: _____

Florist:

Name:_____

Company: _____

Order specified: _____

Free delivery: _____

Price: _____

Deposit due: _____

Directions given: _____

Contract signed: _____

Final payment due: _____

Entertainment:
Name:_____

Company: _____

Length of performance:_____

Overtime fees: _____

Style of performance:_____

Price: _____

Contract signed: _____

Directions given:_____

Deposit made: _____

Specifications about wardrobe, song list, etc.:_____

Final payment due: _____

Resources

(Please note that the following information is for your research use only. The author and the publisher do not personally endorse any service or company.)

For the wedding

Bridal Gowns:
Alfred Angelo: 800-531-1125
Alvina Valenta Couture Collection: 212-354-6798, *www.alvinavalenta.com*
America's Bridal Discounters: 800-326-0833,
   www.bridalgallery.com/bridaldiscounters
Amsale: 212-971-0170, *www.amsale.com*
Janelle Berte: 717-291-9894
Brides-R-Us.com: 800-598-0685, *www.e-brides.net*
Christos: 212-921-0025, *www.christos.com*
E-Brides.net: 800-598-0685, *www.e-brides.net*
Emme Bridal: 281-634-9225
Forever Yours: 800-USA-BRIDE
Galina: 212-564-1020
Givenchy: 800-341-3467
House of Bianchi: 781-391-6111
Impressions: 800-BRIDAL-1

Jasmine Collection: 630-295-5880
Jessica McClintock: 800-276-1835
Jim Hjelm: 800-686-7880
Joya Designs: 800-642-6504
Kleinfeld: 888-383-2777, *www.kleinfeldbridal.com*
L'Amour: 800-664-5683
Lili: 626-336-5048
Manale: 212-944-6939
Martin McCrea: 800-424-2976
Melissa Sweet Bridal Collections: 404-633-4395, *www.melissasweet.com*
Michelle Roth: 212-245-3390, *www.michelleroth.com*
Mon Cheri: 212-869-0800
Mori Lee: 818-385-0930
Pallas Athena: 818-285-5796
Carol Peretz: 516-328-7271
Priscilla of Boston: 617-242-2677, *www.priscillaofboston.com*
Private Label by G: 800-858-3338
Signature Designs: 800-654-7375
Silvia Designs: 760-323-8808
Simple Silhouettes: 212-598-3030, *www.simpledress.com*
St. Pucchi: 212-840-3164
Sweetheart: 212-947-7171
Tadashi: 800-533-2117
Tomasina: 412-563-7788
USA Bridal: *www.usabridal.com*
Venus: 818-285-5796

Bridesmaids' Gowns:
Alfred Angelo: 800-531-1125
Bianchi: 800-669-2346
Bill Levkoff: 800-LEVKOFF
Chadwick's of Boston Special Occasions: 800-525-6650
Champagne Formals: 212-302-9162
Entourage: 212-719-0889, *www.ebridesmaid.com*
Fashion: *www.fashion.net*

Galina: 212-564-1020
JC Penney: 800-527-8347, *www.jcpenney.com*
Jessica McClintock: 800-276-1835
Jim Hjelm: 212-764-6960, *www.jimhjelmoccasions.com*
Macy's: 877-622-9274, *www.macys.weddingchannel.com*
Melissa Sweet Bridal Collection: 404-633-4395, *www.melissasweet.com*
Simple Silhouettes: 212-598-3030, *www.simpledress.com*
Spiegel: 800-527-1577, *www.spiegel.com*
Thread Design: *www.threaddesign.com*
Watters and Watters: 972-575-9884

Tuxedos:
Gingiss Formalwear: *www.gingiss.com*

Children's Outfits:
Belle of the Ball: 818-952-8111, *www.belloftheball.com*
Joan Calabrese: Available at many children's stores
Pat Kerr: 800-901-5223
Serafina: 212-253-2754, *www.serafina.com*

Shoes and Handbags:
Kenneth Cole: 800-KENCOLE
Dyeables: 800-431-2000
Fenaroli for Regalia: 617-723-3682
Nina Footwear: 800-23-NINA
Shoe Buy: *www.shoebuy.com*
The Sak (handbags for bride and attendants): 888-THE SAK1,
    www.thesak.com
Watters and Watters: 972-960-9884, *www.watters.com*

Veils and Headpieces:
Dream Veils and Accessories: 312-943-9554, *www.dreamveilsacc.com*
Fenaroli for Regalia: 617-723-3682
Homa: 973-467-5500, *homabridal@aol.com*
Renee Romano: 312-943-0912, *www.Renee-Romano.com*

Invitations:

For additional savings of up to 30%, contact Informals at 800-6-INVITE with the catalog book and model number of the invitation you like. This company offers discounts on retail invitation sales.

Anna Griffin Invitation Design: 404-817-8170, *www.annagriffin.com*

Botanical PaperWorks: 888-727-3755

Camelot Wedding Stationery: 800-280-2860

Cranes: 800-572-0024, *www.cranes.com*

Embossed Graphics: 800-325-1016, *www.embossedgraphics.com*

Invitations by Dawn: 800-332-3296

Julie Holcomb Printers: 510-654-6416, *www.julieholcombprinters.com*

PaperStyle.com (ordering invitations online): 770-667-6100, *www.paperstyle.com*

Papyrus: 800-886-6700, *www.papyrusonline.com*

Renaissance Writings: 800-246-8483, *www.RenaissanceWriting.com*

Rexcraft: 800-635-3898

The Precious Collection: 800-537-5222

Rings:

A. Jaffe: 800-THE-RING

American Gem Society: 800-346-8485, *www.ags.org*

B&N: 800-358-6223

Bashoura: 800-876-0829, *www.bashorainc.com*

Benchmark: 800-633-5950, *www.benchmarkrings.com*

Bianca: 213-622-7234, *www.BiancaPlatinum.com*

Chris Correia Collection: 212-695-4711, *www.chriscorreia.com*

Christopher Designs: 800-955-0970

DeBeers: *www.adiamondisforever.com*

EGL Gemological Society: 877-EGL-USA-1, *EGLUSA@worldnet.att.net*

Honora: 888-2HONORA

John Christian: 888-646-6466, *www.ringbox.com*

Keepsake Diamond Jewelry: 888-4-KEEPSAKE

Lieberfaub: 800-241-2991, *www.liberfaub.com*

Novell: 888-916-6835, *www.novelldesignstudio.com*

OGI Wedding Bands Unlimited: 800-578-3846, *www.ogi-ltd.com*

Paul Klecka: 888-P-KLECKA, *www.klecka.com*

Rudolf Erdel Platinum: 212-633-9333, *www.rudolferdel.com*

Scott Kay Platinum: 800-487-4898, *www.scottkay.com*

Steckbeck Designs: 800-845-8423

Tacori: 800-421-9844, *www.tacori.com*

Wedding Ring Hotline: 800-985-RING, *www.weddingringhotline.com*

For information on how to design your own wedding rings, check out *www.adiamondisforever.com*.

For information on how to order Family Medallions, the sterling silver or gold over silver symbol pendant given to the children of the bride or groom, call 800-237-1922.

Bridal Shows and Conferences:

Great Bridal Expo: 800-422-3976, *www.bridalexpo.com*

Limousines:

National Limousine Association: 800-NLA-7007

Organizations:

Association of Bridal Consultants: 860-355-0464

American Federation of Musicians: 212-869-1330

American Rental Association: 800-334-2177

American Society of Travel Agents: 703-739-2782

Better Business Bureau (to find the Better Business Bureau of your state or locale): *www.bbb.org/bureaus*

Professional Photographers of America: 800-786-6277, *www.ppa-world.org*

Wedding Web Sites:

Bride Again Magazine: *www.brideagain.com*

Bride's Magazine: *www.brides.com*

Della Weddings: *www.dellaweddings.com*

Elegant Bride: *www.elegantbridemagazine.com*

Martha Stewart Living: *www.marthastewart.com*

Modern Bride: *www.ModernBride.com*

Our Beginnings (offers invitations and stationery at 40 percent off): *www.ourbeginnings.com*

Our Big Day (create your own wedding announcement Web page):
  www.ourbigday.com
Premiere Bride: *www.premierebride.com*
The Best Man: *www.thebestman.com*
The Knot: *www.theknot.com*
The Wedding Channel: *www.theweddingchannel.com*
The Wedding Helpers: *www.weddinghelpers.com*
Today's Bride: *www.todaysbride.com*
Town and Country Weddings (upscale): *www.tncweddings.com*
Ultimate Internet Wedding Guide: *www.ultimatewedding.com*
Wedding Bells: *www.weddingbells.com*
Wedding Central: *www.weddingcentral.com*
Wedding Details: *www.weddingdetails.com*
Wedding Spot: *www.weddingspot.com*
Wedding USA (wedding information listed by state): *www.weddingusa.com*
Wedding World: *www.Weddingworld.com*

Wedding Registries:
Bed Bath and Beyond: 800-GO-BEYOND, *www.bedbathandbeyond.com*
Bloomingdale's: 800-888-2WED, *www.bloomingdales.com*
Crate and Barrel: 800-967-6696
Dillards: 800-626-6001, *www.dillards.com*
Fortunoff: 800-777-2807, *www.fortunoff.com*
Gift Emporia.com: *www.giftemporia.com*
Home Depot: *www.homedepot.com*
JC Penney: 800-JCP-GIFT, *www.jcpenney.com*
Macy's Wedding Channel: 888-92-BRIDES, *www.macys.weddingchannel.com*
National Bridal Service: *www.weddingexperts.com/nbs*
Neiman Marcus: *www.neimanmarcus.com*
Pier 1 Imports: 800-245-4595, *www.pier1.com*
Sears: *www.sears.com*
Service Merchandise: 800-582-1960, *www.servicemerchandise.com*
Target's Club Wedd Gift Registry: 800-888-9333, *www.target.com*
The Gift: *www.thegift.com*
The Wedding List: 800-345-7795, *www.theweddinglist.com*

Wedding Network (Internet wedding registry): 800-628-5113, *www.weddingnetwork.com*

Williams Sonoma: 800-541-2376, *www.williamssonoma.com*

Calligraphy

Petals and Ink: 818-509-6783, *www.petalsnink.com*

Favors and Gifts:

Abbey Press (Christian gifts, bubbles, bells, and other items): *www.abbeypress.com*

Beverly Clark Collection: 877-862-3933, *www.beverlyclark.com*

Chandler's Candle Company: 800-463-7143, *www.chandlerscandle.com*

Double T Limited: 800-756-6184, *www.uniquefavors.com*

Eve.com: *www.eve.com*

Exclusively Weddings: 800-759-7666, *www.exclusivelyweddings.com*

Forever and Always Company: 800-404-4025, *www.foreverandalways.com*

Gift Emporia.com: *www.giftemporia.com*

Godiva: 800-9-GODIVA, *www.godiva.com*

Gratitude: 800-914-4342, *www.giftsofgratitude.com*

Margaret Furlong Designs: 800-255-3114

Personal Creations: 800-326-6626

Pier 1: *www.pier1.com*

Seasons: 800-776-9677

Service Merchandise: 800-251-1212

Tree and Floral Beginnings (seedlings, bulbs, and candles) 800-499-9580, *www.plantamemory.com* in Canada, *www.plantamemory.on.ca*

Wireless: 800-669-9999

Paper Products:

OfficeMax: check your local listings

Paper Access: 800-727-3701, *www.paperaccess.com*

Paper Direct: 800-A-PAPERS

Sparks (paper and card store): *www.sparks.com*

Staples: 800-333-3330, *www.staples.com*

The Wedding Store: *www.wedguide.com/store*

Ultimate Wedding Store: *www.ultimatewedding.com/store*

Wedmart.com: 888-802-2229, *www.wedmart.com*

Weather Service:
AccuWeather: *www.accuweather.com*
Rain or Shine (five-day forecasts for anywhere in the world, plus ski and boating conditions): *www.rainorshine.com*
Weather Channel: *www.weather.com*

Wedding Items (toasting flutes, ring pillows, etc.):
Affectionately Yours: *www.affectionately-yours.com*
Beverly Clark Collection: 877-862-3933, *www.beverlyclark.com*
Bridalink Store: *www.bridalink.com/store2*
Magical Beginnings Butterfly Farms (live butterflies for release): 888-639-9995, *www.butterflyevents.com*
The Sarina Collection: 888-6SARINA, *www.sarinacollection.com*
The Wedding Shopper: *www.theweddingshopper.com/catalog.htm*
Treasured Moments: 800-754-5151, *www.treasured-moments.com*

Wine and Champagne:
Wine.com: *www.wine.com*
Wine Searcher: *www.winesearcher.com*
Wine Spectator: *www.winespectator.com*

Beauty Products and Services:
Avon: *www.avon.com*
Beauty.com: *www.beauty.com*
Clinique: *www.clinique.com*
Elizabeth Arden: *www.elizabetharden.com*
Eve (carries Lorac, Elizabeth Arden, Calvin Klein, and more): *www.eve.com*
iBeauty: *www.ibeauty.com*
Lancome: *www.lancome.com*
Mac: *www.maccosmetics.com*
Revlon: *www.revlon.com*
Sephora: *www.sephora.com*

Self-Care and Health:
To figure out your healthy weight range for your wedding day: *www.phys.com/go/bmi*
Cyberdiet: *www.cyberdiet.com*
Dance classes online (free!): *www.bustamove.com*

Drugstore.com: *www.drugstore.com*
E-Fit: *www.efit.com*
Fitness Online: *www.fitnessonline.com*
Mother Nature: *www.mothernature.com*
Tufts University Nutrition Navigator (for healthy eating tips):
  www.navigator.tufts.edu
Vitamins.com: *www.vitamins.com*
WebMD (to compile your family's health history): *www.webmd.com*

For the honeymoon

Airlines:
Air Canada: 800-776-3000, *www.aircanada.ca*
Air France: *www.airfrance.fr*
Alaska Airlines: 800-426-0333, *www.alaskaair.com*
Alitalia: *www.zenonet.com*
Aloha Airlines: 800-367-5250, *www.alohaair.com*
America West: 800-247-5692, *www.americawest.com*
American Airlines: 800-433-7300, *www.amrcorp.com*
British Airways: 800-247-9297, *www.british-airways.com*
Continental Airlines: 800-525-0280, *www.flycontinental.com*
Delta Airlines: 800-221-1212, *www.delta-air.com*
Hawaiian Airlines: 800-367-5320
KLM Royal Dutch Airlines: 800-374-7747
Northwest Airlines: 800-225-2525, *www.nwa.com*
Southwest Airlines: 800-435-9792
TWA: 800-221-2000, *www.twa.com*
USAir: 800-428-4322, *www.usair.com*
United Airlines: 800-241-6522, *www.ualservices.com*
Virgin Atlantic Airways: 800-862-8621, *www.fly.virgin.com*

Discount Airfares:
Cheap Fares: *www.cheapfares.com*
Discount Airfare: *www.discount-airfare.com*
Priceline: *www.priceline.com*

Cruises:
Cruise Lines International Association: *www.cruising.org*
A Wedding For You (weddings aboard a cruise ship): 800-929-4198
American Cruise Line (East Coast): *www.americancruiselines.com*
American Hawaii Cruises (weddings aboard a cruise ship): 800-474-9934
Carnival Cruise Lines: *www.carnival.com*
Celebrity Cruises: *www.celebrity-cruises.com*
Cunard: *www.cunardline.com*
Delta Queen: *www.deltaqueen.com*
Discount Cruises: *www.cruise.com*
Disney Cruises: *www.disneycruise.com*
Holland America: *www.hollandamerica.com*
Norwegian Cruise Lines: 800-262-4NCL, *www.ncl.com*
Princess Cruises: *www.princess.com*
Radisson 7 Sevens Cruises: *www.rssc.com*
Royal Caribbean: 800-727-2717, *www.royalcaribbean.com*

Resorts:
Beaches: 800-BEACHES
Club Med: *www.clubmed.com*
Hilton Hotels: *www.hilton.com*
Hyatt Hotels: *www.hyatt.com*
Marriott Hotels: *www.marriott.com*
Radisson: *www.radisson.com*
Sandals: 800-SANDALS, *www.sandals.com*
Super Clubs: 800-GO-SUPER, *www.superclubs.com*
Swept Away: 800-545-7937, *www.sweptaway.com/weddings.htm*
Westin Hotels: *www.westin.com*

State and Location Tourism Departments:
Tourism Office Worldwide Directory: *www.towd.com*

Train Travel:
Amtrak: 800-872-7245, *www.amtrak.com*
Eurailpass: *www.eurail.com*
Orient Express hotels, trains, and cruises: *www.orient-express.com*

International Cottages and Villas:

Country Cottages (cottages and villas in the U.S. and Europe):
800-674-8883

Interhome (allows you to search for chalets or villas abroad by specifying
your price range, type of accommodations, nearby tourist sites, special
needs, and more): *www.interhome.com*

Index

style, basic elements of, 147-148
Referrals,
    getting, 31
Registry, bridal, 141-143
Rehearsal, wedding 197-206
    arranging the processional at, 200-201
    dinner after, 204-206
        do's and don'ts at, 205-206
        exchanging gifts at, 205
        planning the, 204-205
    organizing the, 197-198
    practicing the ceremony at, 201-203
    practicing the recessional at, 203
    starting the, 199-200
Responsibilities,
    of best man, 70
    of bridesmaids, 69-70
    of maid/matron of honor, 69
    of ushers and groomsmen, 71
Rings, wedding,
    designing your own, 122
    designs of, 120-121
    engraving of, 122
    for children, 123
    groom's, 121
    information sheet for, 265
    shopping for, 123-124
    trends in, 120-122

S

Seating,
    at reception tables, 254-255
    chart, 253
Shoes, styles of, 107-108
Shopping, comparison, 31
Shower, bridal,
    appropriateness/propriety of, 139-140
    guests for, 141
    registries for, 141-143
    types of, 140-141
Songs, selecting, 163-165

Spouses, former, invited to wedding, 46
Stress,
    coping with, 216-223
        activities, 222-223
        alternative medicine, 222
        aromatherapy, 220-222
        exercise, 218
        intimacy, 222
        massage, 220
        meditation, 219
        proper nutrition, 216-217
        sleep, 216
    sources of, 215

T

Tests, medical, 77
Tiaras, bridal, 106
Transportation,
    cost of, 173-174
    for guests, 176
    options for, 174-175
    shopping tips for, 175-176
Trends, second wedding, 24-25
Tuxedo,
    information sheet for, 264
    renting a, 117

U

Ushers,
    gifts for the, 226
    responsibilities of, 71

V

Valentine's Day, wedding on, 49-50
Veils, bridal, 105-106
Vendors,
    dealing with, 34
    unscrupulous, 29-30

About the Author

Sharon Naylor is the author of 14 books, including *How to Plan an Elegant Wedding in Six Months or Less*; *The Mother of the Bride Book*; *The Bridal Party Handbook*; and *1001 Ways to Save Money and Still Have a Dazzling Wedding*. She is the wedding budgeting expert for Bridal Guide magazine and a regular contributor to *www.njwedding.com*.

She has written often for *Bride's*, *Bridal Guide*, *Woman's Day*, *Self*, *Cosmopolitan*, *Shape*, and other national magazines. She is co-author of the holiday novel *The Ornament*, which will benefit Mothers Against Drunk Driving (MADD).

Sharon Naylor is a member of the highly prestigious Author's Guild and The American Society of Journalists and Authors. She has won top honor awards from *Writer's Digest* magazine and the Academy of Motion Picture Arts and Sciences.

She lives in East Hanover, New Jersey and is currently at work on her next wedding title.